BONADEA'S BOOK OF EVERYDAY ENCHANTMENTS

ABOUT THE AUTHOR:

Patricia deSandro has served the Pagan community for decades, working within the wisewoman/shamanic and Romano-Celtic traditions as healing facilitator, elder, and high priestess. Her knowledge of wild herbs and healing ways came from the teachings of an Amish farm wife, a Cherokee elder, a wisewoman healer, a witch queen, and a conjure man. She blended their wisdom with the teachings of her spirit contacts and her own gifts to develop her unique spiritual path. BonaDea has been teaching and presenting rituals and workshops in many places throughout the country for public and private events since 1990. In 1999, she founded the Circle of the Sacred Grove Temple of the Old Religion as an initiatory coven. BonaDea is also a storyteller as the character, Granny Root, sharing her original fairytales as teaching stories with children and adults. She devotes her time to her ever-growing family, her writing, her community and her painting.

FOREWORD BY H. BYRON BALLARD

PATRICIA DESANDRO

BONADEA'S BOOK OF EVERYDAY ENCHANTMENTS

Chicago, IL

Paperback ISBN: 978-1-964537-48-1
Library of Congress Control Number on file.

Published by:
Crossed Crow Books, LLC
518 Davis St, Suite 205
Evanston, IL 60201
www.crossedcrowbooks.com

Printed in the United States of America.
IBI

Dedication

I dedicate this book of enchantment to my children, grandchildren, and great-grandchildren who embody incredible magic. They are the reason I write.

Acknowledgements

I wish to thank my parents who instilled a love of books from the very beginning and my children and dear friends for building my confidence and keeping me on task. I also wish to thank my author friends who encouraged me time and again to get those words on paper and the Crossed Crow Books team for taking a chance on me.

TABLE OF CONTENTS

PREFACE

From as far back as I can remember, I could see and communicate with spirits of all kinds. As a young child, I would come up with little rhymes and songs with these special friends. This I kept a secret. My special gifts were not looked on favorably by the church or my family. When I reached the age of puberty, I set it all aside. Then, when I had children of my own, that awakened the magic once again in me. I didn't have to hide it anymore. I pretended I was only entertaining my children, but I was serious about the magic. Together, we talked with fairies, animals, and plants, with the storms, the sun, the moon, and the stars. Oh yes, and rocks and trees!

I eventually discovered this was an actual spiritual path that embraces the ability to do those things. After many years of training, mastering my skills as a wisewoman and high priestess, I have accumulated many rhymes, spells, and charms that I have created and that have been very successful for me. I have shared some of them, one by one, over the years with loved ones, but now, in my golden years, I would like to share them with all of you. May they inspire you to create your own!

FOREWORD

Many of us find ourselves abiding in places not of our making—too many chores, far too much stress, fear and anxiety pulsing through the workaday world. When we were little, folklore and fairy tales taught us to expect the unexpected and to meet all challenges with courage and pluck, behaving in ways that are honorable and kind.

That is not a bad way to live, if you think about it. Especially the plucky part.

BonaDea never lost that childhood sense of wonder and she offers it here to her readers set on a silver tray, with cups of tea and pretty cakes, too. Her book is a banquet of the magic that is within each of us and permeates the world around us. The beautifully simple magics in this book will delight you and remind you that the world—your world—is filled with enchantment.

Not only that city park and the cherry tree in the neighbors' pasture, but also in your favorite thrift store or while driving to see your best friend. True magic is everywhere and by the time you reach the end of this book, you will be able to harvest magical energy and use it simply and effectively.

BonaDea models one of the most important parts of magical practice by her invitation to all of us to engage our creativity in pursuit of these helpful tools. We understand that she had mentors and teachers, that she sometimes uses spells learned years ago but the best parts of her magic—revealed again and again throughout these pages—come from her imagination. She has written each one of us a permission slip to be free to try things that may originate in our daydreams, in our childhood memories or in our sojourns into the Land of Night.

The author reminds us that such journeys into the heart of the world need not be undertaken alone. We can certainly learn from and work with others, as she has done. We can also find companions along the way, as we revert to that enchanted time of adventure and lore. These companions can be friends or family but they may also join us from the natural world. Land spirits, ancestral spirits and the devas of the plant kingdoms are waiting for us to recognize them and come into a sweet relationship, filled with delight.

I envy you this first step into the deepest and broadest lands of enchantment, lands made manifest through your birthright as a child of Magic and through the pages of this thoughtful, well-wrought book. Pack your smallest bag with a stone from your garden, snacks from the pantry and your feral curiosity. Everything else you will find along the way.

I promise.

H. Byron Ballard

INTRODUCTION

The purpose of this book is to share the magic I have found in words, gestures, the natural world, and everyday objects. It is strictly based on my personal experiences. All of the rhymes, spells, chants, and songs presented here are from my own mind and hand. I learned mostly by doing and paying attention to lessons from Nature and Spirit, and a few trusted elders.

Of course, I have been influenced by many people in my life, both intentionally and serendipitously. In the past, I have used a few of their spells and enchantments with success, along with many traditional charms, some of which are hundreds of years old, but I find I prefer to use my own. Why? Because I make them up on the fly. I create them in a moment of need. This approach works best for me; plus, it is fun and gratifying to take advantage of the energy and momentum of the moment and have the words, gestures, rhymes, and rhythms pop out of my head and heart spontaneously…as if by magic! I also have the advantage of the support of all the alliances I have made and the knowledge of how to make new ones (more on these techniques later).

This is not to say traditional incantations aren't valuable. They are. While personally created spells use the energy of the maker driven by the energy of the moment and the energy of the need, traditional spells are infused with the energy of all those who have successfully used those incantations since the time they were created. That can be a lot of power! One of the downsides of that, though, is those spells came from someone else's need and might not line up perfectly with your situation or goal. You could use it as is and hope the Universe understands what you want, or you could tweak it to fit your needs. But, if you are going to do that, you might as well just create your own and call on the assistance of your allies and ancestors to help manifest it.

Another downside to using traditional spells correctly is that you might need environments or tools that are not immediately available to you. Also, you would need to have the words and gestures memorized or have them written down right next to you. That, of course, means having a grimoire. There is definitely magic in that alone! However, for everyday needs, do you really want to lug around your Book of Shadows everywhere you go? I found that very awkward and cumbersome, myself.

The older I get, the more I go back to what I learned as a child from the fairies in my father's garden: *you can find magic in the most peculiar places. It's all around you and even inside you!*

This book is designed to inspire you to use your imagination and life experience to create your own magic. Throughout this book, there are questions for you to think about and spaces for you to write your thoughts, ideas, and experiences.

PART I

WILL YOU BE MY FRIEND?

Creating enchanted relationships with our world, both natural and manmade alliances.

I see the Divine in everything. That spark from Source, the Divine Consciousness, I believe is contained in every cell of everything that exists, every molecule of this planet. That spark is what drives the motion of the atoms. That spark is the energy that holds things together. This divine energy is interactive on different levels. Energy speaking to energy, life speaking to life. This is truly the basis of my magical work. Whether I'm recruiting a stone or thanking a stick, I am communicating with spirits and aspects of divine energies, whom I call the gods.

I was taught that I should only work with objects directly from nature or made from natural things, that those are the only things that will hold and respond to energy. In these modern times, however, we are presented with many other choices. What about all the synthetic materials scientists have come up with? I agree, making them is damaging to our planet. But now, they exist as part of our world. Synthetic plastics, for instance, are made from natural gas, coal, and crude oil. All of which come from ancient, decayed matter consisting of plant and animal (including human) remains. Overwhelmingly processed, sure, but the original molecules are still there. The same molecules that were once part of our ancestors.

The Snow White Effect

Imagine you are wandering through a bucolic scene with a song on your lips. Flowers burst into bloom and turn their faces toward you as you walk by. Birds sing with you as they hop and flutter from branch to branch, keeping up as you stroll along. Deer, rabbits, and other creatures raise their heads in acknowledgement as you acknowledge them. Trees smile down on you. The sun shines, a gentle breeze blows.

An enchanted scene, for sure, reminiscent of Disney's *Snow White*. While this is the stuff of fairy tales, there is big truth to the general concept at play here.

The scene just described illustrates the concept of making allies. It has been my experience that if you have made the effort to connect with these different beings in nature and stayed consistent with reinforcing those connections, it is probable that those creatures would be drawn to your energy and respond with theirs, even the trees. They have such big auras and can easily attach to yours, pull you in closer, and share their energy if there has been frequent, loving contact between you and the tree. Loving intent and consistency are the most important aspects of this process. Expect it to take a while. Just as when you meet a new person, a good solid friendship takes time to develop. Children are so natural at this! I believe this is because they approach life with unconditional acceptance until it's taught out of them.

Unconditional acceptance, in my opinion, is the definition of unconditional love. It is the acceptance of each creature just as they are. That they aren't something we can change. Also, they have a right to exist on their own terms. Once we can accept a creature without judgment, I have found that they will reciprocate in kind. This is building an alliance. Much magic can happen when working with your allies, whether it be for protection, healing, or prosperity.

1) It Has a Soul

Enchanting a thing in the fairytale world means bringing that something to life, with energy you create, to be a companion or to help you in some way. It becomes an ally and always has your back as long as the relationship remains strong. This requires respect and responsibility from the enchanter for the ally. In fairy tales, if the person betrays or disrespects their ally, they will be abandoned by it and, in some cases, punished. There is a large kernel of truth in this.

When we enchant something in our world, we have imposed an *intent pattern* (more about this later) that we have created onto the pattern of something else. That something else now follows the intent of our pattern. We have given it a soul, so to speak. In essence, it is now alive. If we do not respect that, we are effectively cutting ties with that ally, and it will no longer serve us. Then, we will suffer the consequences.

For example, if you buy a car you really like and give it a name and talk to it, you have enchanted it to be your ally. You have *ensouled* it. You have given it a purpose and declared the terms of the agreement; "I'll take care of you, if you take care of me." If you accidentally forget to get gas one time and the needle is on empty, and the nearest gas station is forty miles away, then you sweet-talk your car and state what you need, that you will get to that station. If you have built a good relationship with your car, you are in agreement with its energy pattern and it with yours. Chances are, you will make it to that gas station, even if your car is running on fumes.

Your continued positive responses to the car's needs and treating it like a friend keeps the enchantment going. You are feeding the energetic intent pattern of the car's existence that you have created. If you neglect and abuse the car, there is a dysfunctional connection where the car's physical pattern begins to break down because it has lost its soul. Then, there is no way it will be there for you when you really need it. I am sure we all have experienced this in one form or another.

My Sanctuary

I have white doves made of paper and plastic hanging in and around my home. They symbolize peace to me. I also have a chunk of quartz crystal hanging in the tree outside my door to siphon off unpleasant energy from anyone coming to my front door. Between that tree and my door, there is also a large chunk of rose quartz that is programmed to radiate loving energy to replace that yucky stuff that was siphoned off.

All of the items in my home have been chosen and enchanted to promote an environment of comfort and peace, especially for myself and my dog. This kind of enchantment is just telling the objects what I want them to do. When I clean my house, I remind each object of their designated tasks to recharge their energy. When I water my bonsai palm tree, I tell it how much I enjoy its leaves and how it adds life to my living room, even in the dead of winter. I tell my bed how much I appreciate its comfort and longevity. I remind my sofa that when people sit on it, I want them to feel at home and content.

My life is full of allies like this, like my friend, the lightbulb. It has been with me through several years and three moves and still works. I thank it every day for giving me light when I need it and I keep it dusted. Enchanted allies make such a difference. To be in agreement with things we take for granted is a magic all its own.

Do you have any ensouled objects in your day-to-day life?

2) Friends in High Places

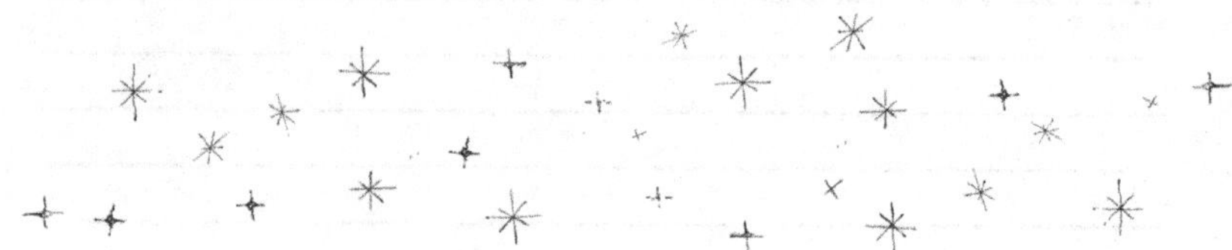

When we develop a relationship with a non-human living being, like an Elemental spirit, a fairy, an animal, or a plant, the agreement is a little different. They have a life force and a will of their own. They have their own evolving intent patterns. We introduce ourselves to each other. We each decide if we want to be allies. We each come to the table with an offer of friendship based on how we define it. Sometimes, negotiations are required. Promises are made and trust is established. It becomes a contract we wouldn't want to break. They are our equals; we have no dominion over them. Great affection can develop over time and betrayal can bring pain. But these relationships can be unbelievably rich, it is a profound privilege to have one.

Out in the Elements

Sometimes, the initial contact comes from them. Those who don't require a physical body will make their presence known by altering your immediate environment in unusual ways, such as the Elementals, the spiritual essence or energetic beings of the elements of Air, Fire, Earth, and Water.

Air Elementals, for example, might get your attention by creating a breeze that only you can feel or creating the scent of flowers only you can smell. Water Elementals could appear as a wave at the beach, reaching out and tugging on only you in an unusual way. Fire Elementals could appear as a flame leaning out from a bonfire, following or mimicking your movements around the fire, especially if you are singing, chanting, dancing, or drumming. Earth Elementals can distract you off a trail to show you something hidden, like a rare plant or a small cave. They also might make an unusual looking stone appear in your path right before your eyes and compel you to give it to a stranger. These are examples of what I have personally experienced over the years.

The Elementals I am referring to have traditional names, reportedly from Paracelsus, a Swiss alchemist from the sixteenth century. They are Sylphs (Air), Undines (Water), Gnomes (Earth), and Salamanders (Fire). I have found, though, that *they* will tell you what to call them when you have developed a relationship with them.

If any of them make themselves known to you, they might want you to do something, like the aforementioned giving a stone to a stranger. For instance, if the waves at the beach keep depositing trash literally at your feet, the Elemental might be asking you to help them by cleaning it up.

I have noticed that, if I acknowledge the interaction by greeting the Elemental and doing what they ask or leaving an offering of some kind (more about this later), they become allies by giving me protection or warning of their element's wild side, or by assisting me with something in a way only they can.

Here is an example. One night, several years ago, I took some women to a small clearing in the woods to do a full moon ritual. It was cloudy, but there was very little chance of rain. As we were setting up, rain started. The women who had come with me complained we would have to cancel, but I had alliances with Water and Air. I told the women to quickly get in the circle we had just cast. I stood in the middle and said with outstretched hands,

Creatures of Water! Creatures of Air!
Let no rain fall on those who are here!
In our circle around and about,
Along the path, and in and out!
As our will, it is done!

The rain slowed and stopped almost immediately. We thanked Water and Air, finished gathering our things, and performed our ritual. The moment I ended the ritual, the clouds opened up and the rain drenched us! When I spoke the incantation, I had been holding the image of us staying dry during the set up and the ritual. I hadn't included the thought for the rain to hold off until we were loaded up again and safely back in our cars!

I recall another incident with the element of Water. During my priestess training, our instructor taught us how to call up rain. We set the parameters for a small shower, just at our location, to last a short time. We raised the rain. It worked. This was on a Tuesday evening. We met for class every Tuesday at 7:00 p.m. Several weeks later in class, one of the students asked if the rest of us had noticed it was raining, and that it had rained every Tuesday evening since we called the rain! We had neglected to limit the working for only that one class time. We quickly did a counter working by telling the element of Water to only rain when Earth needed it.

This was an excellent lesson in being mindful of how one sets intent and following it through. Though I strongly advise you lovely readers to leave weather-working alone. Anything you might do in that regard affects more than just you and your immediate area. When we try to make changes to the weather, we are interfering with climate patterns that are beyond our understanding because we are not able to see the bigger picture. Better we should focus our energy work on adapting to whatever weather our planet gives us.

Stone and Sea, Flame and Wind

The following visualizations can help you understand the elements as they manifest in our plane of existence. Each one can be used as a meditation by itself. Please note how each element is modified and influenced by the other elements. The verse at the end of each visualization calls up the spiritual essence of the element as an ally and how it works within us. Each verse can be used separately as needed for affirmation or as a call for a specific strength. They can also be used all together as a ritual of revelation and connection between the elements and self. Following each visualization is space for you to write how you relate to each element.

The visualizations were developed during successive meditations as I focused on each element. The verses came to me as I took a long walk with my dog one morning. That is my time to get myself in a good mindset for the day and process new concepts more thoroughly. Here, I combined these verses with the visualizations for each element. Together, they are great for strengthening one's resolve and reinforcing elemental alliances.

Stone

Take a deep breath, close your eyes, center your focus. Travel now on your breath into your imagination. If you have a hard time doing that, pretend you can and just focus on the words.

Find yourself on a small ledge near the peak of a mountain... you are clinging to the rock face with all your might! Feel your body merge with and become the *stone*. You feel like you have been a part of this mountain all your life and you are content. You love the crisp cleanness of the thin, dry air. You love the sun shining warmly on you and the wind in your face. You even love the snow and ice that blankets you when the temperature falls below freezing. You especially love the rain, washing you clean as it pours off you in little waterfalls.

But wind, rain, ice, and heat are driving a wedge between you and the peak, fracturing your connection to the mountain rock, *earth* solidified. As erosion loosens your grip, you remember how you got there.

A million years ago, you were pushed up with Earth's expanding heat, a molten mass from deep within Her womb, up from the darkness and heat into cooler, brighter air in a dramatic birthing event that changed the face of you and Earth. Now you are being separated from Her! You finally release to gravity and free-fall down, down through the air until you bounce on a narrow ledge littered with other pieces of broken stone. You, however, have momentum, and you roll to the edge and over it, bumping, sliding, leaping down the now gentler slope of the mountain you were once a part of. There seems to be a rhythm to this movement, and you give into it, allowing it to carry you onward. You bounce and roll between trees and boulders that have found a home where the land becomes flat. You come to rest at the edge of a lake. You are now sheltered in the shadow of the mountain, but erosion will still wear you down, even here.

The grasping waves of the lake made by harsh, stormy winds reach out and rock and roll you into a new rhythm. The water scrubs your surface, rounds your corners, and dulls your edges, washing you away one molecule at a time. The grains of sand rub against you, seeming to say, "We were once like you, and you will become like us."

After a few hundred years or so, you have succumbed, and sand, you are. Miniscule pieces, sometimes dry and hot, sometimes sloshing with the waves, but always moving, shifting, mixing with small pieces of bone, decaying leaves, fish scales, and the debris of other earthly creatures left behind from one transition or another. Odors and textures blend as the wind and water stir the organic soup of life and death.

Layer upon layer, you and others like you are pulled under the wet sand. The pressure of waves and debris and time compresses you, pulling you in tighter and tighter. You seem to finally stop moving, but you are still changing. You are mud, now. You feel the pressure of many footprints against your pliable surface. Your molecules join together as if holding hands. Denser and denser you become, trapping tiny puddles of water in your air pockets into which your mineral content condenses and grows crystals, sparkling jewels that you hold in secret.

You are solid and hard and strong, now. You have combined with the particles of many other things, and you hold the history of life within your structure. You are aware that you are a part of a bigger whole again, a part of Earth. You have manifested in many forms, and you are not finished yet.

Deeper and deeper, you sink below the constantly thickening surface. You are still becoming, still transforming, as deep underground rivers sculpt your body into ethereal shapes and hollow you out into caverns. Wise entities, the spirits of your existence, often referred to as Gnomes, the Knowing Ones, guide and support your journey through time.

Many stories you hold within your depths: stories of mountaintops and trees, sun and wind and rain; stories of life forms that slithered, crawled, and walked over you or burrowed through you. You yearn to share your experiences and all that you have witnessed. Deep within your caves, you whisper your journey as wind and water echo your voice. The Gnomes hear them, and they know where your secret jewels are hidden. They protect your secrets.

Still deeper you sink over time, until you feel the beat of Mother Earth's heart. You have returned to Her womb, and you sense another birth about to happen. The heat builds and melts you, transforming you back into red-hot magma. You remember, now, that once you lived on a mountaintop, and you will again. You have returned to your source as all earthly life does. The relentless, challenging forces of erosion and gravity, what seemed to be your enemies, have fulfilled your deepest desire to return and reconnect. Surrender to the volcanic birth and feel yourself being thrust upward to be part of a mountain again. Once more, you feel the wind and rain and sun!

Now, you also feel the gentle rhythm of your own heartbeat and breath. Feel the awareness of your arms and legs return. Pull that awareness out of the surrounding rock and back into your body. You still feel you are somehow connected to the mountain, because you are. You are but one variety of the combination of the same minerals that manifest as the mountain, the sand, the mud, the bedrock, the Earth. Your body responds to the same forces and influences that shaped this planet. You follow the same rhythms. You are an integral part of the greater Earth Matrix.

Take a long breath and walk down the mountain on a gently sloping trail. Pause on a flat slab of rock. As you pause there, the magnetic pull of Earth strips off the energetic sludge you have collected over time, pulling it down to be recycled in Earth's womb.

Now call the element of Earth to rise up through your bones, strengthening you.

I call to the power
Of the Earth beneath my feet!
Rise like a mountain to the sky.
Steady me, steady me!
Firmly on the bedrock I stand.

Shift and move Earth through your body from bone to bone. Give thanks to Earth.

Sea

Take three breaths. Now imagine yourself on a narrow beach in a little sheltered cove at the edge of the *sea.* It is a beautiful sunny day, with a blue sky and whipped-cream clouds. You walk to the water's edge, feeling the warm sand beneath your feet. The gentle, lapping waves touch your toes.

The sea invites you in and you start walking on its sloping, sandy bottom until *water* is up to your shoulders. You hear gulls calling above your head and you notice the scent of the sea on the breeze. You feel so relaxed and comfortable that you lay back and float. You don't swim, just float. Water supports you completely. The sun warms you from above and the sea is cool beneath you. You start to lose awareness of your arms and legs as you identify more and more with the undulating surface of water. You no longer feel your body's edges, but you feel the sea's edges, the shorelines and the sandy bottom and the air on top. Within your belly, fish are swimming.

There is another awareness that stretches you out further into the strands of water; the streams and rivers that flow into you and out of you, connecting you to lakes and ponds. You are all one, though you have different characteristics. You slide effortlessly between your boundaries, exploring, connecting, flowing, seeking a balance of all your surfaces.

The sun continues to warm you, and your surface yearns to get closer to the source of that warmth. Your molecules move rapidly to separate, dissipate, and evaporate. You feel yourself floating upward now, through the warm air. There, up high, your particles find each other in the atmosphere and congregate. Together you float in the breeze as fluffy white clouds, the strength of Air holding you up.

Some of your clouds drift over high mountains where the air is cold. There, your molecules stick together in delicate crystalline shapes that fall to build glaciers below. The glaciers flow too, like solid rivers, ever so slowly seeking to reconnect with the sea.

Denser and denser your warmer clouds become as they move from the mountains across flat land. More of your molecules gather and soon you are shadowy and heavy. You are too heavy for Air and your particles clasp each other and form droplets, falling down, down as rain. Your drops separate the threads of sunlight between the clouds into the glistening colors of the rainbow.

The first to catch your drops are the uppermost leaves of a tall tree. The weight of you bends the leaf down and you slide off to the next leaf where you pause as an insect takes a drink. From leaf to leaf, you slide and dribble until you reach the ground where you puddle up between leaves of grass and tree roots. There, a part of you sinks into the soil, nourishing the plants and mixing their debris to make mud. A small frog splashes in the puddle of you, making miniature waves that remind you of being the sea.

You yearn to stretch out and join the rest of you between the edges of the shorelines, seeking to balance your boundaries with Earth and Air. The spirits of your wild essence, the Undines, whisper the way to you. As more of you gathers in the puddle, you become strong enough and big enough to reach outward in a new rivulet going toward the sea. As you glide along, a deer steps out from the trees and laps her rough tongue against your surface, pulling some of you inside her.

Sliding under grass, around pebbles, pushing grains of sand, you flow your way toward home. Combining more puddles along the way, your body expands into a swiftly flowing river, creating new boundaries to contain you while the Undines take on shapes in your foam.

Finally, through the power of your flow, you reach the sea. You feel embraced as you spread out and reconnect with the rest of you. It is dusk now and the full moon is rising, reflecting in your undulating surface and tugging on your body.

Some of your fish jump, breaking your surface and sending ripples outward toward the shore. A leaf on a low-hanging branch at the edge of the shore dips in the evening breeze, starting ripples in the opposite direction. The patterns of ripples cross each other and create a network of designs that repeat and change over and over again, ricocheting back and forth. Part of you rests in a protected lagoon, where your surface is smooth and still. Here, you are a mirror, reflecting back to the world things seen and unseen, mysterious messages of life.

You gradually become aware of your human edges again as the night cools you down. Pulling your awareness back into your human boundaries, you drop your feet down and stand once more on the sandy bottom. You walk out of Water and up onto the beach.

Even though you are dry now and standing on solid ground, you feel you are still connected to Water. This is because you are. Water is suspended throughout your body, nourishing and cleansing, just as in the insect, the frog, the deer, and the plants. You contain the rivers, the lakes, the seas, the rain. You flow with the tides and reflect the life around you. You seek balance.

Take a long breath. Stretch your arms as the wild essence of Water pours over you like a waterfall, washing away remnants of old sorrows. Deep breath. Now call up Water and move it through your body.

I call to the power
Of the Waters running deep,
Rise like the tide beneath the moon,
Come balance me, come balance me!
Flowing like a river through my soul.

Shift and stretch your body to give it space to flow.
Give thanks to Water.

Flame

Take three breaths. Now imagine yourself standing in a cozy cottage. It is darkened by evening shadows, but you can make out a cushiony chair by the light of the *fire* coming from the stone fireplace. You settle comfortably into the chair. The dancing *flames* fascinate you and as you gaze at them, you are drawn into their beautiful colors.

Fire, flickering to a rhythm you can't quite understand, hypnotizes you, and your consciousness climbs into the flame. You don't feel the heat as you did from outside of the flame, but you do feel a vibration. It courses through you in waves, making you pulse with energy. You feel its great passion and desire for its own existence! It accepts what is available to it with gusto and devours it! There is great joy in being alive! It is then that you realize you are inside a living creature. You wonder about its life. You wonder about its birth and death.

Fire invites you to dance. As you begin to move, you start to understand the rhythm and you hum. No longer are you aware of arms and legs, just the stretching of your energy into the wood beneath you and the air above you. You pull the essence of the wood upward into your belly to be consumed and the wood beckons you to go deeper into it. The wood gives itself to you as it is overcome by your passion. It will be transformed into a new substance, known as ash, that fertilizes the growth of new life when gifted to Earth. This is one of the gifts of Fire.

Reaching your fiery fingers into Air, you pull yourself up as if to reach the heavens, your flames gulping oxygen so you can continue your dance of life. Your frenzy creates an aura of heat that ripples the air around you, constructing a matrix for mirages and visions. There is an elemental symphony that accompanies your dance. Your vibration hums. The wood pops and crackles as it is transformed. Water suspended in the wood hisses as its molecules are released into Air. Air, stirred by the dance, whispers.

Your dance is over now. The wood is almost gone. You sink down and focus your diminishing energy inside the remaining wood. Wriggly, brightly glowing shapes of Fire essence, the fiery Salamanders, crawl along the edges, making a path for you. A dull, reddish-orange glow is all that is left visible, but your vibration is still there, pulsing within the old boundaries of the wood. Your aura is still there, too. You are still alive, and you must finish your work. By morning, your gift of ash is all that remains.

You find yourself back in the easy chair and you marvel at your experience. But your journey is not yet over, Fire has many lives. As you sit by the now cool, dark fireplace, pondering, you hear a distant rumbling from outside. You walk out the door and see in the distance a lone tree in the middle of an empty field.

Beyond the tree, you see large, billowing, dark clouds moving across the sky. There is a tingling quality to the air, like electricity. Suddenly, a blinding flash of lightning splits the clouds, followed by a thunderous boom. The tree receives the fiery bolt and bursts into flames. You just witnessed the birth of Fire and the death of a tree.

The sounds of the fire sing to you, and an image forms in your mind of an ancient ancestor carrying a burning branch from a lightning-struck tree back to his family to keep them warm and to cook their food. This is another gift of Fire.

Fire continues to sing to you and images of transformation shimmer in its aura, images of forest fires and burning buildings, images of explosions and volcanoes. Mass destruction! Then, you see little seedlings and saplings thriving in the burned-out forest, in the ash-fed soil, finally having space to grow and having access to the light and warmth of the sun. You see images of redesigned buildings and parks being built stronger and safer in place of burned-out rubble. The flames also show you visions of new mountains, valleys, and islands where none existed before. Mass transformation! Now you realize that you have been transformed by Fire, as you become aware of your human body once again.

But what about the deaths of so many creatures caused by Fire? All that Fire touches is transformed. The death of any creature is a changing from its form into its spirit essence that can be born again into a new life. Energy lives on indefinitely.

Fire is like you. It is born of a spark of energy. It breathes the air and feeds on substance to stay alive. It can sleep for a while, in the ashy debris as embers, and then it can wake up again, once stirred and fed. It waxes and wanes, and it dies.

We have Fire within us. It is the energy that keeps us going. It warms our body from the inside. It inspires and compels us; it drives us to survive, and it encourages us to dance our joy.

The flames die down, their dance ending once again. Take a long, slow breath as you gaze at the flickering embers. Allow spirits of Fire, the glowing Salamanders, to gently crawl over the edges of your body now, to singe away vestiges of doubt and apathy. The Salamanders energize you with confidence.

Call up Fire into your belly to reignite that divine spark.

I call to the power
Of the Fire deep in the Earth!
Rise like a flame from molten core!
Burn in me, burn in me!
Feed the spark of courage in my heart!

Move with the flame as it reaches higher, invigorating every portion of your body. Give thanks to Fire.

Wind

Take three breaths. Pause. Find yourself standing on a hill with wildflowers scattered through the tall grass. Tall mountains are in the distance behind you and at the foot of the hill is the edge of the sea. The day is sunny and pleasant, and the breeze caresses your skin. White, fluffy clouds drift high above you. *Air* carries the songs of birds and the delicate scents of flowers. It undulates over the grass, mimicking sea waves. You look up toward the clouds and you see a hawk gliding on the thermal of air currents, gazing back down at you. He seems to be asking you to join him up there.

You feel yourself rising off the ground, as if the breeze, with airy hands, is lifting you. With your arms outspread like wings, you balance yourself on the column of warmer Air rising up from the ground. With no effort, you spiral upward, swirling into cooler Air. You can look down as the bird does and see the treetops. You see the uppermost leaves dancing in the breeze. The hawk speeds up and swoops down, thinking to catch a meal in the grass. You keep up for a while, but decide you would rather be Air. Air doesn't concern itself with food. Air seems to have no boundaries or rules. Freedom!

You lose a sense of your body's form as you feel yourself expanding, contracting, pushing against anything that might try to contain you, and surrounding, embracing, caressing anything that is willing to dance with you.

You are Air. You are free-flowing molecules and sparks of energy that have escaped the grasping hold of Earth and Water. You carry oxygen, among other things. You are the product of gaseous transformation. Heat makes your particles move faster, expanding and rising and swirling. Cold makes them slow down, contracting and sinking and releasing. The essence of Air spirits, the Sylphs, guide you to where you must be. They manifest here and there, more felt than seen, arranging and rearranging the energies you carry according to what is needed.

You are the Great Carrier. You carry gifts of pollen to female flowers. Creatures small enough to seem invisible take advantage of your flowing ways to colonize new territories. Butterflies ride gently on the edges of your currents, tracing your meanderings around the wildflowers. Birds and insects beat their wings against you, pushing themselves along as if rowing in a stream. Seeds with built-in parachutes lift off from their mother plants and let you carry them to faraway places to start a new life.

You are the Great Messenger. Feel the sounds of music, language, and life resonating on your waves of vibration. You take fragments of thoughts, words, and images from mind to mind, from the ancestors to the future, inspiring the creative and informing the seekers. You bring scents to both prey and predator alike, communicating danger, food sources, availability of mates, and location of territories.

You are the Mighty Cleanser. Blowing through neglected places, you scatter dust and cobwebs and bring fresh new energy. You carry away the invisible debris of life; pollution, toxins, and gases, replacing it with fresh, nourishing substance. You carry more and more until you are full and heavy. Now, you hover in low clouds over cities, trapped by the weight of your burden. You are no longer able to move your currents of energy to circulate warmth and coolness. You have no choice but to release your poisonous burden back down to Earth with the moisture that is also trapped within you, making acid rain.

You are the Mighty Mover. Over the oceans, rivers, and lakes, you blow gusts that push Water out against its edges. You make ripples that grow and expand to waves. When you blow over land, trees sway while soil and sand change their patterns. Sometimes you swirl with great speed and power, enlisting Water as a partner, moving across the land and sea as tornadoes and hurricanes, clearing away all that is in your path while you roar. Like a mighty invisible hand, you wipe away the old to make room for the new.

You are the Great Sculptor. You blow relentlessly against mountains, wearing down the sharp edges as you release particles of stone from their surfaces. Ever so slowly, you reshape the landscape. Through holes and crevasses started by Water, you help to hollow out magnificent caves and hidden passageways.

You are the Atmosphere. You surround Earth with protection and sift stardust to replenish Earth's supply of minerals. You carry within you all that Earth needs to survive. You ebb and flow but have remained the same since you were created. You have been the breath of dinosaurs and the breath of humans and will be the breath of the future. You hold the tools of manifestation and destruction on many levels. You are the aura of Earth.

You have drifted and blown all around Earth and now you have returned to the hilltop meadow, brushing against the tall grass. You sense an edge to your energy in the now still Air and realize you have returned to human form.

Pause as the wild energy of the wind picks up again. Face into it as it blows through you, clearing the dust and cobwebs from the deep corners of your mind.

Call up the element of Air to fill your lungs.

I call to the power
Of the Air that I breathe!
Rise like a gently blowing wind.
Fill me, fill me!
Bring clarity of vision to my mind.

Move as the breeze is blowing through you from the inside. Give thanks to Air.

What has been the most profound experience you have had out in the elements of nature?

3) Twilight Friends and Lords of Place

Inhabitants of the Fairy Realms (which include many types and races), I have noticed, interact a bit differently. Some people are more aware of them than others. Those people are said to have the 'sight." Occasionally a fairy will appear to a person unexpectedly, usually in their peripheral vision or in the dimness of twilight and dawn. My experience tells me these beings are all around us, but in another dimensional reality. Sometimes, welcoming gestures and offerings will encourage them to come into your awareness, but regardless of who initiates it, the first meeting is clearly on their terms.

I will pause here to share some information about offerings to non-human living beings. An offering is, obviously, a gesture of friendship. It could also be a token to seal a treaty or a contract. Proof of bond. The offering needs to mean something to you besides being something the other being wants. Grabbing any old package of cheap or expired cookies off the shelf for your fairy contact might not be well received. The offering must have value to the giver as well as the receiver.

In the past, traditional offerings were milk, butter, honey, wine, or bread, to name a few. These took effort on the part of the human. Milk came from the effort of milking a cow or goat that had to be raised and fed. Butter was made from milk, and churning the butter took time, patience, and muscle. Making bread required growing and grinding the grain, then making and baking the bread. A tremendous amount of work! Wine was made from fruit that had to be grown, processed, and aged, and honey had to be searched out and then gathered at great risk to the gatherer.

I have done some of those things, so I can attest to the value of those as offerings! In these modern times, these items can be purchased from the local grocery store. So, unless you had to walk ten miles to the store to buy them or paid an exorbitant amount of money beyond your limits for them, they really aren't that valuable. And cheap, easy offerings don't carry any of the giver's energy, effort, and sweat.

Why are those three things so valuable to the receiver? Because the giver is, in effect, giving a part of themselves for the good of the relationship, and that is what we want to expect from them. Plus the fact that those offerings contain not only energy from the giver, but also some of the giver's DNA. Now, the being has a way of identifying and remembering the giver and can bond with their energy pattern in a more complete way. Remember the old way of sealing a deal between two people by spitting in their respective hands then shaking those hands with each other? Exchanging DNA, pattern bonding with pattern. To become blood brothers or sisters, the palms of the hands were cut so their blood mixed. Exchanging DNA, pattern to pattern.

That connection is serious and powerful. So, in today's world, a food item you made yourself would be a good offering. So is singing a song, especially if you wrote it yourself. That takes time and energy. And for them, DNA can be gleaned from your breath while singing. Playing a musical instrument specifically for them works, too, especially if you wrote the music. So does a favored piece of jewelry you wore often or a cherished and frequently worn item of your clothing. Something you crafted yourself is an excellent offering. It is definitely a gift of a part of yourself!

But there has been more than one occasion when a gift was accepted and taken before giving was even considered!

Let me tell you about an incident. Many years ago, I lived right at the edge of a little wetland woods. I walked down the trails almost every day. However, I had yet to make a formal alliance with the woods. This was several months after I started my coven, Circle of the Sacred Grove. I had created a pendant, from clay, of a tree that symbolized our coven members' connection to each other. I wore mine every day and I would unconsciously reach up and finger it if worrying or pondering something.

One particular day, I was walking through the woods and realized I had wandered off-trail. I reached up for my pendant and it wasn't there. The chain was still there and so was the bale (the little piece that held the pendant on the chain). How could the pendant have come off if the bale was still closed? I searched for that pendant until dark, to no avail. At that point, I asked the woods to make it visible so I could find it. Didn't happen. For the next few days, I searched those woods. Nothing. At that point, it finally occurred to me that the spiritual essence of the woods had wanted it and took it. I asked for it back, then demanded it back. No luck. We hadn't made an alliance yet.

I finally realized this was a conscious attempt to get my attention. This was something I had made. It contained my DNA and plenty of my energy. If I agreed the woods could have it, I would be participating in an alliance. I also realized that I could make another one for myself, so I agreed. It seemed as if the Spirit of the Woods was blessing the Circle of the Sacred Grove by wanting to share in that image. The spirit or combined essence of everything that lives in a particular place is often referred to as the *Lord of Place, Guardian,* or *Egregor.* I understood that's what this entity was. I never saw that original pendant again. It belonged to the Spirit of the Woods.

A few nights after this experience, I had a dream that part of the woods rose up out of the ground, exposing the long tree roots as legs, the treetops for a head, its midsection a mass of soil, moss, and stones. It was shedding small clumps of dirt and pebbles. It slowly walked out of the woods and into the street by my house. The neighbors ran screaming, but I was not afraid and stood there looking up at its massive form. It paused right by me, and I climbed up to stand among the moss and ferns on its back. I held onto the trunk of one of its saplings as it turned and went back into the woods. I woke up. The Spirit of the Woods had shown itself to me. I learned much from this Egregor over the years. It taught me how trees communicate and where to find glow-in-the-dark mushrooms. It showed me where the very rare Green Dragon plant grows, and other secrets. I made a promise to keep the Woods free of trash and not divulge its secrets as my part of the alliance.

Not too long after that, I went into the woods with a small herb-cutting knife that my husband had made for me. I had found some wild plants I wanted cuttings of. I walked down one of the trails to the place where these plants were growing. I reached for my knife which was tied to my belt (so the Woods wouldn't claim it) and it wasn't there. The cord was still knotted to my belt. I called out to the Spirit of the Woods and said I wanted my knife back. No response. I looked for it for three days. On the last day, I told the Woods I wanted it back because my husband had lovingly made it for *me.* No response. I gave up.

A few days later, I was in the woods tearing down construction tape kids had used to tie some saplings together. A shaft of sunlight broke through the leaves and shone on the intersection of two trails a few yards from me. I glanced over and there was my knife, lying right in the center. I went over and picked it up as I thanked the Woods for returning it. At that moment, a very deep but quiet, echo-y voice said, right in my ear, "Do not cut or harvest any living thing in these woods. Take only what is freely given." I readily complied. Those were the Egregor's terms of our alliance. As time went on, the Woods gave me anything I needed willingly.

Do you think you might have had an encounter with someone from the Fairy Realm? Or an Egregor? What was magical about it?

4) Where True Magic Lives

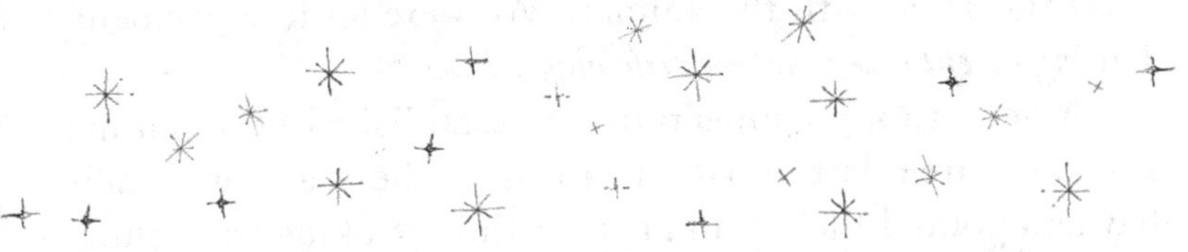

I don't think I have to tell you animal lovers how profound animal alliances can be. The loyalty, adoration, and pure, unconditional love given to us by our animal companions is unsurpassed. But I have a couple of stories I want to share with you.

When my husband and I and our three small children moved to our little Indiana farm far from town, our main goal was to be as self-sufficient as we possibly could. This was the 70s and we were part of the hippie back-to-the-land movement. This meant raising our own food. We wanted our children to know where our food came from. But we were city people, and even though my husband and I read book after book, we really didn't know what we were getting ourselves into. It was quite an adventure, let me tell you! We planted fruit trees and a vegetable garden. We had goats for milk, chickens for eggs and meat, sheep for wool, geese, ducks... and a pony for the children (wink, wink). I talked to the seeds when I planted them and talked to the plants as they grew, telling them I would feed and water them and then they would feed my family. Our little children helped where they could. I did the same with the animals. We were all in agreement. *Loving acceptance is where true magic lives.*

A very strong connection was established between me and our three dairy goats. I talked to them as I got their hay and poured their grain. I spent time stroking their shiny coats. Sometimes, I would sing to them as I milked. I would sit out in the meadow and watch them graze when I needed to take a break. They would occasionally come up and nudge me. Our agreement was, I would make sure they had a good life, a grassy meadow, good grain, and a cozy barn and they would share their milk with my family (their offspring always got first dibs). That relationship went so deep, I found myself telling them about my life while lying in the straw with them at naptime.

When my favorite goat was struggling with a breech birth and the vet was too far away to come help, I had a talk with her, literally eye to eye. This was going to be a first for both of us. I told her what was wrong and that I needed to go in and turn the baby around if they both were to survive and that it would be painful. I told her I needed her to stay still. She didn't break eye contact, just nudged my hand, then remained motionless while I turned the baby and delivered him. Communication, love, and trust between friends. This is magic.

The chickens...oh, my wonderful chickens! Our agreement was I would give them a great life, good grain, free range, and a cozy barn. As with the goats, I spent time watching them and learning their ways (roosters are quite entertaining, by the way). I talked to the hens when collecting eggs and when scattering corn for them in the yard. They would give me eggs and new chicks. And then, after some time, their bodies would feed my family. Easy to say, but very difficult to do. This was one of the biggest, most profound learning experiences of my life. I am sharing it with you here, because it was full of magic and unconditional love on a huge scale.

We wanted our children (and ourselves) to know and respect the fact that the food we ate came from living beings, plants and animals. Chicken doesn't just come prepackaged from a grocery store. I asked an older country woman in our area to teach me how to take the life of a chicken so they wouldn't suffer and how to honor their profound gift to our family. She told me to choose the one that would do the feeding and spend some time lovingly talking to it.

I told the rooster I had chosen about how I enjoyed providing him with everything he could want. He had free run of the farm, many hens to keep him company, and we fed him the best grain. Now, it was his turn to feed my family. I told him how thankful we were that he would provide us with nourishment. I told him how much we would honor his great gift to us. I have to tell you, I was crying. He stood quietly in my hand, looking at me. After some stroking of his beautiful feathers, I told him it was time.

I walked him to the tree stump where my friend was sharpening the knife. He didn't try to fly away. I laid him down on the stump and he voluntarily stretched his neck out. I hesitated in utter amazement. If he had fought against it in *any* way, I wouldn't have been able to go through with it. But now, I couldn't deny his great gift of sacrifice. A single, swift, sure stroke provided a painless death for our rooster. I witnessed his spirit leave his body and fly away to be reborn into another life. The family all helped with preparing dinner that evening and we said a special thanks for our rooster. This is magic.

I learned that life and death have many meanings. I learned that communication between souls in any form is possible, if done with unconditional love and understanding. I learned that every act of eating requires the death of something. Therefore, the one who will be eating must honor the sacrifice of the other to keep the cycle of unconditional love going. I believe this applies to *any* life form, plant, animal, or other. Everything on earth lives in a cycle. When we die, our remains will feed the land that feeds us. This is magic.

I wrote this little chant or prayer to be used when any creature dies, for any reason, animals, humans, even plants. This is my prayer when a friend passes on. I use it to honor the source of food about to be eaten. I said it for our rooster. I also say it when I see an animal killed on the road. While speaking the rhyme, I imagine the animal/human/plant as it was when alive and looking at me as I express my gratitude. This is respecting and honoring my allies.

Thank you for the gift of your life now passed.
May your next life be better than your last.
Release to the light, blessed spirit.

What was the most profound interaction you have had with an animal?

All the Creepy Crawlies

Well, it helps if they are your allies, too. But I must tell you, I am still working on this concept myself. I have had some great successes, though, and I will share those with you here.

As I have written earlier in this book, I spent many years living at the edge of a wetland woods. So, you can imagine all the insects I have met. The female mosquitoes lie in wait just inside the tree line for the next warm-blooded creature to come by so they can get some blood to make their eggs. Nobody wants to be that creature! But mosquitoes have a right to exist, especially in wetland woods. When I walked the trails, I was in their home. It took me a minute to figure out that nothing was going to stop them from feeding in their own home.

So, I talked to the females one day (while standing outside the tree line, of course) and told them I was a mother, too, and I understood how important it was to have what you need to have healthy babies. I also told them they carry diseases that would be very harmful to me, and I wasn't willing to put myself at risk to let them feed on me. Plus, the anticoagulant they inject when they bite makes me terribly itchy. I added that if they bite me, I would defend myself and they would probably die as a result. I came up with a little charm I would say just before entering the woods:

Hello mosquitoes (or any other insects)!
I respect you and intend you no harm.
Allow me to pass with no harm to me.

Well, it worked, and we negotiated the agreement that they would not bite me if I said this before I entered their realm. But if I stood still for more than two minutes at a time, I was fair game. As long as I followed this agreement, I was never bitten. They didn't even fly around me. But if I got involved with looking at a flower and stood still for too long, they would remind me, but they never swarmed me.

I was so pleased with how well this worked, I decided to use it with ants. I must say, I admire their sense of community, their stamina, and their durability, but...they just really freak me out! Not to mention the pain of a zillion fire ant bites! There were several species of ants in and around our place near the woods. If I happened upon them, I would say this little charm and they would stay away from me while I worked in my garden.

Spiders. I am learning to get along with them. I suffered greatly from multiple spider bites one time. It was clearly my fault...I was cutting down weeds in an overgrown area that had many hidden spider nests without checking there first. And I was wearing shorts. But living next to woods with a high population of spiders the size of my hand, I thought it important to make friends with them. My introduction to these woodland spiders was rather abrupt. I opened the shed door, and one jumped out of nowhere and landed squarely on my chest! Her legs spanned the length of my hand. I gasped, of course. She looked as startled as I was. After a moment (seemed like an hour) of me not taking a breath, she hopped back off and disappeared. I soon discovered several in the rafters of the shed. I was afraid to open the shed door!

I had been taught a Native American spider song. I thought maybe if I sang it softly as I opened the door, then maybe the spiders would like it and leave me alone. I tried it and it seemed to work. After doing that several times, I decided I would try to make up my own spider song because I didn't really know what the words meant in the Iktomi song, and I wasn't Native American. So, I did. It worked just as well, maybe better because I created it and that makes a difference when trying to make an alliance with a creature. I sang softly, thinking my voice might be too loud for them. My song was very quiet and slow. A little spider lullaby.

Spider, oh, spider,
This is my little song for you.
I want to be your friend
So you won't have to bite me
And I won't have to squash you.
You have such beautiful long legs

And such pretty markings on your back.
Listen to my song.
I hope you like my song.

I sang this song as I slowly walked through the shed to get my tools. None of them moved an inch. The next day, I decided to try it again, figuring that if I did that, the spiders would get to know me. I went out to the shed and slowly opened the door. There was one very large female sitting just on the inside of the door, eye level with me.

I was already singing my spider song, so I sang even more softly and inched closer to her. I was standing about a foot away, and I reached up and laid my hand on the door about a foot from her. As I continued to sing to her, I slowly slid my hand closer and closer along the door panel. She didn't move a hair. I could feel all the other spiders in the rafters focused on me and I tried not to picture all of them jumping down on top of me. I just kept singing. I was able to get my hand right up against her feet. She never moved. Her span went from my fingertips all the way down to my wrist. Seven inches! I was touching her feet! It occurred to me that the steady vibration of my voice was calming to her and all the others. An alliance was made right there and then. I wouldn't squash them or startle them, and they wouldn't jump on me or bite. I would sing to them, and they would keep the shed free of unwanted visitors, including other insects. I never had a problem with them after that, all the years I lived there.

One summer, I went whitewater rafting in West Virginia with some friends. At one point, in a calm spot on the river, we decided to take a break. We pulled off to the side where a rocky outcropping provided a place to jump off and swim. It was really hot that day. As I was starting to step out of the raft, it slid away from the rock. I reached up to find a handhold on the side of the rock to prevent myself from falling. I found a tiny ledge and pulled myself up out of the raft. When I stood up and looked to see what I had grabbed hold of, a bunch of little glittery eyes were staring back at me! Of course, I yanked my hand away. Our guide informed me I had found a fishing spider lair. The same kind of spider that lived in my shed! Big, soft, and fuzzy. I started humming right away. Even though I had startled the spider, it didn't harm me.

What has been your most memorable experience interacting with an insect?

5) Some of My Friends Are Deeply Rooted

You never know when you might need a friend, and that could mean more than just a human friend, or even an animal friend. Plants can be friends, too. My wisewoman teacher, Linda Diane Feldt, urged me to talk with wild plants. If I was not feeling good, the plant that would serve my needs would make itself known to me.

This is important to remember. Once you think a plant is offering to help you, in whatever way, do your research. Check it out thoroughly and consult with experts. Spend time getting to know the different aspects of the plant before you use it. Take your time. It is worth the effort.

As you can probably figure out by now, it would be beneficial to get to know a variety of plants before you need them. Elaine Fischer, the Amish farm wife who was my first teacher of wild herbs, used to take me on walks around her farm and mine, randomly pointing out which plant did what. At first, I thought, "Oh, okay, I'm getting to know her, and she likes wild plants." I think it was the second time exploring the meadow with her, I realized she was teaching me important information! I started bringing a small notebook with me so I could write down everything she said for future reference. That was in 1977. I still have that little notebook. That was the year when the magic in me that had been slumbering for so long started to wake up again.

Nice to Meet You, Peppermint!

I was learning how to intentionally make alliances with the plant world. My wisewoman mentor told me to spend a year getting to know one plant. I chose peppermint. I learned to recognize it in the wild, learned its growth cycle through the seasons, ate it, dried it to make tea, used it to settle my stomach, and sniffed it to help me stay alert and focused. And, of course, I talked to peppermint. I asked it to show me what it needed to keep it healthy. I sat with it and ran my hand through it. I greeted it each time I gave it water. Every time I used peppermint, I thanked it for serving my needs. I learned how to listen to it, too, by observation and meditation. Peppermint became my equal partner when I needed it. I was impatient, though, and a year seemed like a long time. But looking at the bigger picture, a year just starts the process of making a plant alliance. Like having a human friendship, one is always learning something new about the other. Everywhere I have lived after that, peppermint would grow without me planting it. I have many plant allies now and I treasure each one.

Let Me Help You

There are times when one's body (or soul) needs certain nourishment from a certain plant. If the person lives in one location for a time, the plant that can help mitigate the problem often starts to grow, unbidden, in the person's yard or garden. When I started having hot flashes and mood swings, a "weed" started growing in my flowerbed by the back door. It grew tall very quickly and was in the way when we tried to use the door. I pulled it up and it grew right back. At one point, after we had been away from home for a week, I found it pushing its slender branches between the outer and inner doors. It seemed it wanted to get into the house! Its persistence was a little unnerving! I took a leaf and a flower to my wisewoman teacher to see if she knew what it was. She told me it was motherwort, a medicinal plant used to treat hot flashes, mood swings, and other symptoms of menopause. It soon became one of my most loved plant allies. I gave it its own special place in my garden.

Another plant ally experience happened when my husband shattered his leg in an industrial accident. Though the doctors managed to put his leg back together, they couldn't seem to get a handle on the swelling. I looked through my notes from my various wild plant teachers to find something that might help. Then I remembered the plant, burdock. I had used it as a poultice once a long time before, to soothe a second-degree burn on my daughter's hand. I thought maybe it might help soothe my husband's leg, even though it's not known to help with that. So, I went outside to find a burdock plant, to no avail.

I went to the Spirit of the Woods and said that I needed to find some burdock to make a poultice to help my husband. I didn't feel any resistance, so I searched the woods and only found one small burdock plant. I took just a few of the leaves. I thanked the plant and the Spirit of the Woods and made my poultice. Within a day's time, the swelling had started to go down. I had enough leaves to last another two weeks, but I was going to need more. I went out to the woods again a week or so later and to my surprise, there were several new burdocks starting to grow right along the edge of the woods bordering our property!

One can get a lot of information from books and other people about plant allies. But, taking the time to build a personal relationship with certain plants will allow one to find out how the plant will interact with *them*. Again, like in human friendships, each one is unique to those involved.

Fruits and Veggies

When I was small, I remember apologizing to the raspberries as I was stealing them from my dad's garden. I told them I was sorry I had to eat them, but they just tasted so good! The bushes seemed okay with it because they kept producing more!

A major part of my wisewoman training was learning that all plants have purpose and personality, and if we want the optimum relationship with them for food consumption, we need to communicate that. So, I talk to any fresh produce I have before I eat it and when preparing dishes, I talk to each ingredient and tell them what I want them to do. I enchant them. I am connecting their energy pattern with the patterns of the other ingredients and the food product I am intending to manifest. I am creating a team of nourishment and blessings. Nutmeg, for example, is traditionally associated with success and prosperity. So, I add it to as many dishes as I can for the holidays to give a blessing to those I will be feeding. I usually add cinnamon with the nutmeg, even if it is just a pinch because I think its fiery energy will help activate the blessing of the nutmeg. Here is a cooking spell I use every time I make something in my kitchen.

As I add and stir and mix,
A spell most lovely, I do fix.
Good fortune, health, and love most fair,
Into the pot (pan, bowl) I place with care.
Once, twice, three times 'round,
These three wishes are full-bound!

I enchant each ingredient with intent before I add them. While saying the fifth line, I go around, through all the ingredients, with a spoon, spatula, fork, etc. in a clockwise motion three times.

I wrote this next one when asked to give a blessing for an anniversary dinner with a very large guest list that included people of different faiths. It was so well received; I was asked to do it again the following year.

Divine Grace
Which is in all things,
Bless this food
That it may nourish me (us),
Body, mind, and spirit.
I (we) give thanks
For all whose lives
Made this feast.

What are your favorite plants and why?

PART II

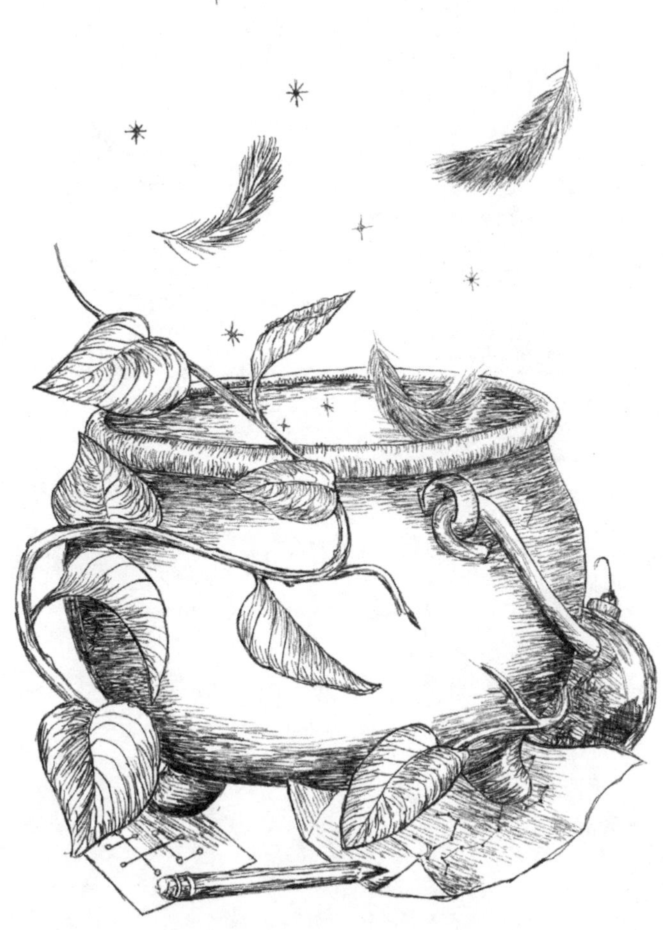

MAKING MAGIC

Grandmothers of the dark,
Grandmothers of the light,
Weave for us a day of beauty,
And a peaceful night.

I start my morning and nighttime prayers with this.

You're So Enchanting!

My working definition of enchant is the use of words, gestures, and sounds to apply intent to affect change. The intent for change is, of course, the most important part. The act of applying that intent is where creativity and imagination comes into play. Words and sound can sharpen the focus and impact of any intent, providing efficient power for the desired result.

The rhythm of how the words are strung together creates a wave of energy that drives the intent toward its target. Alliteration and rhyme create waves of their own, carrying and magnifying the power of the intent. These three factors also have an effect on the sender. They can filter out distractions from outside influences because these waves of energy promote a light-to-mild trance state within the sender. This creates a clear, laser-sharp path for the energy to affect the desired change. These are the muscles of enchantment.

1) Pay Attention Now

How you word your spells, charms, and enchantments is very important. Though some magical workings can be done without words, most of them need words. Each word is a magical entity all its own and can be used that way. So, putting them together requires diligence. Words cannot be taken for granted, as you will see in the following stories.

Disclaimer: Rhymes and rhythms do not always fall out of my mouth fully developed. Some do, some don't. Well, actually mostly don't. But that's okay. Crafting words is a magical act. One's focus is on the intent the entire time while the effort builds the energies to fuel that intent. The more time and effort taken, the more power is fed into the working. Just be careful while enchanting your work that you don't lose your intent in a deep well of beautiful words.

There's a Word for That

Making up your own words for magical use is not only fun, but triggers a different mindset in you as you use it. It is not tuned in to mundane existence, but a different reality. The energy of the enchantment remains pure without distractions or attachments. No one will know what it means unless you tell them. Therefore, your process and use are protected.

The following enchantment I have used when I want people to gather around me, like when I am ready to do a presentation and people are still milling about or wanting children to settle down in front of me to hear a story. I sing it as I would a lullaby. I sing it over and over, very quietly, until I have the desired result. The sound of my voice, soft and steady, and the rhythm of the words put listeners in a very light trance state, even if they can't quite hear me. They are drawn to the sound but aren't influenced by what the words might mean. It makes them want to listen. Words we can understand can often be distracting because of connotations, feelings, or memories we have attached to them. This process bypasses all that. If your goal is to have them gather, the energy pattern of that intent is conveyed in the sounds, not the words, and is communicated through the unconscious mind.

Gathering In:
Mae low coom-la. (To me please come.)
Moe rah coom-la. (All of you come.)
Neh teel coom-la. (Don't be afraid, please come.)
Mah dahe! (You are all welcome!)

This next one I use to influence people to leave. I use it in the same fashion, but alter my voice into a more staccato sound and deeper tone, still very quietly. It comes across as more commanding but is still done with a smile.

Sending Away:
Low mah ray. (Time to leave.)
Nee mah ray. (Now you leave.)
Teel kah. (With blessings.)

Saying or writing enchantments in a foreign language can have a similar result as creating words. I used Latin, for instance, in this short chant that is part of my morning prayer cycle. It carries me away.

Dea pacem dona mihi.
(Goddess, give me peace.)

Watch What You Say!

When using words to proclaim what you want, don't underestimate their power. You can unintentionally affect others if you are not careful aiming your intent or your target isn't clear. Also, repetition is powerful. Energy is added to the intent with every repeat, especially if you are in any kind of trance state, like during the mundane task of washing dishes or driving a car.

I used to work as a psychic medium at a local psychic fair. There was a fellow reader named David that worked there, too. On my way to work at this fair one day, I kept saying to myself, *I want David to be there today. I really want to get a reading.* I said this many times over as I drove, hoping that it would make sure he was there.

When I arrived, he was not there. I was disappointed but focused on getting ready to welcome clients. My first client was an older man who looked bewildered. He told me he usually drives his wife here, but he never gets a reading. He doesn't believe in them. He didn't know why he suddenly wanted one. I asked his name so we could start. His name was David. I gave him a reading, and he was impressed and left happy.

I had a few more readings after that and then another man

came to my table, again, looking a little confused. He said he had never been here before and wasn't sure what motivated him to come this particular day. I asked his name. His name was David. Hmmm.

The fair was now over, and I was packing up to go home. A young man rushed in and asked me if I could please give him a quick reading. I agreed and he sat down. He looked a little frazzled, so I asked if he needed a minute to catch his breath. He told me he was on his way home from work which included passing by the building we were in. He had seen our sign many times in the past and noticed it today. He said he was never interested in getting a reading before. He thought the whole idea was kind of silly. But today, he felt compelled. He turned so suddenly into the parking lot that he spilled his coffee all over his clothes. He lived just around the corner, so he rushed home and changed and came back. He was confused as to why he just had to have a reading right now, today. I asked his name...David.

Most of my clients are women. I had never had three men come for readings in one day before, let alone all of them named David. Guess my enchantment worked, but not the way I intended!

So, You Want a Pink Cadillac

Here is another story for you with an important message, but this one is fictional. Imagine a guy named Joe had always wanted a pink Cadillac. He thought his life would be so much better if he had one. He would feel happy and fulfilled if he ever reached that goal. He created an elaborate spell to manifest it. The focused energy worked, and he got his Cadillac! Good job! And it's a beautiful shade of pink, too. He drives it slowly around town so everyone can see that he is *somebody* now. Neighbors oohed and aahed and vied for a chance to ride in his new car. After a time, the attention died down. Everyone had seen it, and they all had taken their rides. Everything went back to normal. Now, Joe's unhappy with his life again. He's bored with his new car. He thought his life would be different, but it's back to being the same. He doesn't understand why, after reaching his goal, he doesn't feel fulfilled.

So, what went wrong? Why didn't having a fancy car make Joe feel fulfilled and happy like he thought it would?

It didn't provide happiness and fulfillment because a pink Cadillac is not really what Joe wanted. So, let's walk this back. Joe wanted a pink Cadillac to make him important in the eyes of others. Why did he want to be important? Because he wanted people to notice him. Why did Joe want to be noticed? Because he felt invisible. Why did Joe feel invisible? Because he never felt he was good enough to be acknowledged. This is the core of Joe's need, not the Cadillac. If he had focused his energy on building his self-esteem, his result would have been more fulfilling. He wouldn't be obsessed with having a showy car. He would have a better chance of getting the attention he craved, maybe even a friend or two along the way. And the results would last a lifetime, not just a couple of weeks.

The point of this story is, when you feel you have to have something and you want to work the energies to manifest it, ask yourself why you need that something.

Strip down what you *think you need* by asking yourself *why you need it* until you uncover your core need. Then work the energies for that.

This was not an easy lesson for me to learn. Lots of shadow work and a little trial and error to get there. But I still question what I think my needs are until I reach that core. This makes the difference between failure and success for me. Often, I end up realizing I don't need anything at all. I had just lost sight of what I already had.

What is one of your core needs? How would you address that need?

Finish it!

A spell or charm is an energy pattern that you are creating to accomplish a task. It has two main parts, the statement of what you want and then the command to make it happen. It's like baking a cake. Your intent is to have a fine cake. You gather all your ingredients and mix them together. But all you have is a bowl of batter. You have to put it in the oven to actually end up with a cake and then you must leave it alone while it bakes. You can't keep checking on it to see if it's cake yet, otherwise, it falls (collapses). The same is true for a spell. A charm that finishes the spell, that commands the manifestation, that bakes the cake, is often referred to as a *charm of making*. Once spoken, leave your working alone so it can bake. Because the standard ones (so mote it be, amen, etc.) no longer work for me from overuse, I wrote the following charms of making for myself. I just add one of them onto the end of any spell. Feel free to use them if you like, or, better yet, create your own!

As I say, I see it!
As I see, so be it!

Here are a couple more:

And so it is done!
Now! Manifest!

What's your favorite spell? Try writing it in a different or secret language and add a charm of making.

2) Patterns Everywhere!

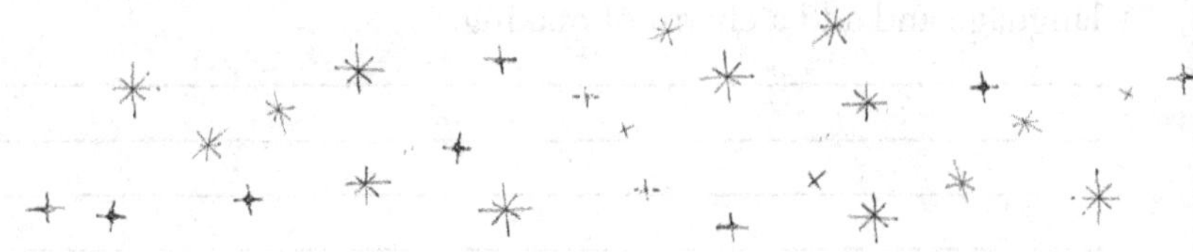

The world is full of invisible patterns. Patterns are the bones of manifestations. We can influence those patterns by making new ones and connecting them. This is how magic works.

Connecting the Dots

Remember those connect-the-dots coloring pages from when you were a child? You drew lines from dot to dot and when you were finished, there was a pattern of lines that looked like something…a dog, let's say. It was just a bunch of dots and lines, but your brain told you it was a dog because the line and dot pattern resembled what your brain knew to be the outline of a dog. Every time you looked at that pattern, your brain reinforced the idea that it was a dog.

So, now you decide to color it to make it look more like the kind of dog you would like to have some day. You do a really good job, so your mom hangs your picture up on the wall. Everyone who sees it says, "Yep, that's a nice-looking dog you got there!"

Your imagination tells you stories of you playing with this dog. Even your family's imaginations might start telling stories about you and this dog.

One day, you come home from school, and there, waiting for you, is a gift from your parents, your very own dog that amazingly looks like the one you colored. What a surprise! But not really. This was an energy pattern at work that manifested a goal, albeit unconsciously.

Here's how it happened. Connecting the dots made a pattern infused by the energy of the action. Being satisfied with how the pattern looked like a dog added more energy because of your acceptance of it. Then, you colored it. Now, it *really* looks like the kind of dog you would have liked. More energy added. Your mom hung your picture up. Now, everyone who saw it commented. Lots more energy added. The dog now had a life in everyone's imagination as your dog. So, imagine you actually came up with a name for this future dog. All that attention aimed at one pattern gave it enough energy that it finally manifested from imagination to the physical world. This is one very simplified example of *intent patterning* and the Law of Attraction. *If you had decided to use the connect-the-dots picture of a dog purposely to manifest one, that action could then be called an enchantment. This is because you would have told (enchanted) the picture to bring you the dog.*

Here is a more detailed example of the mechanics of enchantment and intent patterning. Accept that you are surrounded by little particles of potential energy, too small to be seen, but are waiting to be connected to something and activated. You are thinking you would like to have your own business. You project your thought outward with words carefully chosen to describe your goal. Your words, drawing lines of intention, start to connect with those potential energy particles, virtually connecting the dots to make a picture of what you want.

The lines need energy to turn the thought into reality and the particles need something to do. The lines are "magnetized" by the intention, pulling in those energy particles to create a pattern. The pattern is a blueprint, so to speak, of your goal. The potential energy in each particle now has a purpose. It starts to run along those lines of intention as if they were electrical wires. They are not potential anymore, they are tapped into and connected.

Every time you think of your goal and speak those carefully chosen words, you are sending out more lines to strengthen the connections, building on your basic pattern. The more details you imagine, the more complex the pattern becomes. The intention pattern takes on a life of its own and starts to reach out, looking for other connections to help it go from blueprint to reality.

Now, imagine there is a very successful businessman out there somewhere, looking for a new challenge. He is thinking that he would like to invest in a start-up company and be a coach for a new entrepreneur. His thought draws out lines of intention, connecting energy particles, making a pattern. His goal is to find someone with a business plan who needs his skill set. His intention pattern is open-ended, searching for connections. So is yours. Both patterns are magnetized by their intentions, so they are attracted to one another. When they connect, merging into one larger pattern, the pattern is fed by the continued focused intentions of two people instead of one. Now, the pattern is strong enough to manifest. However, if one of those original patterns is bigger or stronger than the other, it would have a greater influence on the outcome. If either one of the people starts to have doubts or reservations, for whatever reason, their lines of intention start to fall away. This weakens the pattern. It leaves it vulnerable to other patterns with different agendas to attach and sabotage the original intent.

So, how could you make your intent pattern strong enough to manifest? You could use specific words to state exactly what you want and say those words exactly the same way often to reinforce those lines of connection.

By rhyming some of the words and giving your statement some kind of rhythm like in poetry or song, you make your words easier to remember and it adds more power because of the interconnectedness of the words themselves. This is creating a spell. You have enchanted your thoughts to reach out into the universe and bring back your goal. You could use gestures to emphasize the main points, too. If you recite those words at the same time on the same day every week (or any consistent timeframe), with the same gestures, you have created a ritual.

What will your next connect-the-dots picture be about? Draw random dots and connect some of them to make your goal picture and start your enchantment.

My Special Pattern is a Secret

Drawing out your patterns helps you to see what your intent is building. Like a blueprint for your process. Remember the connect-the-dots dog we just talked about? The more places you hang that dog picture, the more energy it absorbs, helping it to manifest. Here is a very effective way to work a spell.

Undo, Make New

My favorite game to play is Bananagrams. I love building words from other words. That is what this is about. First, you deconstruct the word that best describes what you want to get rid of. Then, you find words that start with those individual letters and build a shape with them by arranging them so they all connect by shared letters like a crossword puzzle.

For example, maybe you want to get rid of anger. Print the word out vertically with spaces in between the letters like so…

A
N
G
E
R

Now, write out the words you would like to replace anger with that start with those letters. *Acceptance. Nice, Gratitude. Empathy. Respect.*

ACCEPTANCE
NICE
GRATITUDE
EMPATHY
RESPECT

Notice…the word ANGER is completely gone. Next, arrange those words so they fit together, using shared letters. Think crossword puzzles.

```
   G
   R
EMPATHY
   T
   I
   T
   U
   D    A
   RESPECT
        C
        E
        P
        T
        A
        NICE
        C
        E
```

Now, you have a magic pattern, also referred to as a sigil, that contains the energies of what you want instead of anger. If you draw lines where the words are, you have the same pattern, just without the words. It still holds the energies of the new words. This pattern can be drawn on other things like a piece of cloth you can wear tied around your wrist, on the inside of your shoe, on your hand...you get the idea. It holds a lot of energy because of the time and effort you spent creating this positive pattern by dissembling your anger and creating something different and by focusing on the meanings of the new words.

No one will know what it is, so no one can contaminate your new energy pattern with their opinion. It will continue to work for you as long as you keep it within your personal energy field or intentionally feed it energy consistently.

The Magic Crayon

When drawing out any energy patterns, you could always use crayons. Assign colors symbolic to different intents or different parts of intents. That adds even more power to your workings!

What colors and words would you use for your *Undo, Make New* spell?

3) Safety First

Making safety is an essential skill everyone should master. Being in a safe environment not only protects, it enables the imaginative mind to create. But safety starts inside oneself then radiates outward to influence the larger environment.

Inner Safeness

When feeling scattered or unsafe, I gather up my energy with my hands (or in my mind's eye) and put it all back into my Inner Temple (my place of power/solar plexus). I take a slow, deep belly breath and say the following with another belly breath after. I also do this at the end of meditation and any time I feel the need to mentally escape.

I live in my sanctuary (temple).
My sanctuary (temple) lives in me.

When I was visiting China, I felt very uneasy about the locals crowding against me in the public square. As a rather spoiled American, I'm used to having my personal space. They were not trying to be rude; it was just a cultural difference. The locals had a different understanding of the concept of personal space. They were curious about me, but I didn't know the language and I started to feel self-conscious and unsure of myself. I needed to get my confidence back so I could enjoy my visit. I took a deep breath and came up with this little rhyme to say to myself over and over while pushing my energy field outward a couple of feet and walking through the square. Soon, it seemed people were giving me more space and I relaxed. I started to enjoy them taking an interest in this one American.

This is my sovereign space.
I claim every step I place.

Here is one I use when in clear or perceived danger:

Light is my shield!
Love is my strength!
Power of the Gods,
Defend me!

The Wall

I used to live in a rather scary part of town, surrounded by a lot of crime. It seemed everyone on my block had a big, scary dog. Often, these dogs were unrestrained or were kept in very inadequate fencing. When my little dog and I would take our walks, it sometimes seemed we were running a gauntlet. We both kept a watchful eye out for other dogs, but occasionally one would confront us by surprise. Now, my dog is fearless and would snarl and lunge, ready to fight. But she's only eleven pounds! That's just lunch for some of those big ones! After a few terrifying incidents, I discovered what worked for us. My anger at being afraid of these dogs, knowing they were just doing what they had been programmed to do, motivated me to come up with something that would not hurt them but would protect us.

I created a wall. An impenetrable, opaque, stone wall. I figured if the dogs couldn't see us, they wouldn't go after us. If a strange dog approached us, I would see the wall drop down like a heavy gate between us as I yelled (not screamed) in a deep, commanding voice, "*Wall!*" Once I yelled out, we would be motionless and very quiet. I visualized this wall of solid stone maybe ten feet tall. The dog would suddenly stop, turn their gaze, and look confused. In most cases, they would turn around and go back the way they came. One just sat down and looked in every direction but ours. Once the dog turned fully away, we would resume our walk slowly and quietly, but confidently in the other direction.

Wards and Barriers

A *ward* is something that guards and protects. Anything can be a ward. Anything. It all depends on a strong intent pattern. Even a twig would work if enchanted.

With the help of allies and imagination, you can make a ward in seconds as the need arises. For instance, if being chased in the woods, you could call on the tree roots to trip your pursuer. You could call on the underbrush to obscure or block a path. Of course, you see, having made alliances with trees and other plants or the woods themselves would be an important first step in this case.

When I lived in that dangerous neighborhood I mentioned earlier, I had many wards cast around and in my house. I had wards for the windows and the doors. These, along with locks, protected us. The wards I used included a clear, spherical holiday ornament with dried herbs and small charms, a horseshoe, a paper dove, a toy spider, and a quartz crystal. I had a conversation with each of these about what I wanted them to do. I gave them names. I enchanted them. To me, they were now alive. I fed them with intentional energy every time I laid eyes on them. So, here is how I did that.

"Friend Dove, you represent peace to me. Your job is to lay a sense of peace on anyone who walks through my door."

"Friend Quartz, your job is to siphon off any energy from those who pass this way that would be detrimental to the home I have created."

"Friend Horseshoe on the wall above the door, your job is to be a barrier and make sure no one intending harm comes through that door."

"Friend Spider, you will guard the doorknob."

The ornament with herbs, a friend had made for me as a ward. The contents had already been charged for protection. I hung it above one of the windows and said, "Friend Protector, be a barrier to guard all the front windows against intruders.

You use what you got, make them your allies, and tell them what to do. Then feed them energy periodically.

I have a story for you of how they all worked together to make safety.

One evening, a few years ago, I had unintentionally fallen asleep on the sofa. I hadn't locked the house up for the night, yet. Suddenly, I heard shouting, and I looked up to see people in my front yard. They tried to get in, rattling the doorknob, pounding on my front door and trying to kick it open, yelling, "We know you're in there!" They thought someone was hiding in my house! A fight ensued on my front steps between them as others tried to enter with weapons. Someone threw a metal stool against the tall glass window. They finally stopped when the police arrived.

There were many arrests and injuries among the people outside, *but* the glass window didn't break and *none* of them were able to open the unlocked door. I was absolutely terrified, but my little dog and I remained safe.

I do recommend locking your doors, however. That is the most obvious spell against intruders.

What do you have lying around the house that you can enchant for protection?

4) Making Changes

When we know it's time to evolve but we haven't yet, we can call for help. But first, we need to figure out what we want to change. We know, don't we? But fear gets in the way of moving forward. That's okay. Our need to scale that mountain will soon override our fear and then we'll see it wasn't as big as we thought. Getting rid of old attitudes and looking at the world with different eyes is what usually needs to happen, the rest will come naturally on its own. So, ask for help from your higher self, that part of you that is always in tune with the Divine. The Divine that dwells within you. We all need to be reminded of that at times. If you can't find it, get somebody with experience to help you look for it. But in the meantime, you can say something like this to yourself every morning to get the proverbial ball rolling. I can attest to its power.

I call to the Divine Fire within me
To grow, glow, and burn brightly inside me.
Burn away ego and judgment that harm me.
Bring courage and strength,
Wisdom and grace to fill me.
May the light and love
Of the Goddess shine through me
And bless everything that I see.

Rites of Transformation

These two short rituals are intended to get one unstuck from old habits and move on. The physical act of magical working starts the internal process of making the changes we desire. Then, our job is to maintain those changes.

The Cauldron

This ritual is great by itself or even more powerful with friends. Write down things or situations that really trigger you on separate pieces of paper. As many as you want. Do *not* write down people's names. Only the *issue* you have with them. Light a fire in a proper container, like a cauldron, fire ring, fire pit, barbeque grill, etc. Toss your paper(s) into the fire with great flourish and dance. Really dance! Twirl, stomp, flail! Raise that energy, and every second step or so, push that energy into the fire. Chant until you can't chant anymore! If Fire is your ally, chances are it will react to your energy and flare up with each push. So, be careful and mindful of how close you are to the flame. When you have stopped, take time to feel the release of all that harmful stuff and then stomp your feet or sit down on the actual ground if you can, to ground yourself. If you can't get down that far, sit however you can, but imagine your feet on the bare earth.

Cauldron of Cerridwen,
Anger, fear, and hate within!
Twist and turn!
Turn and spin!
Compassion and truth
Shall rise again!

The Phoenix

This Phoenix ritual is basically used in the same way. Just the intent is a little different. Decide what you would like to change in your life to allow you to become who you want to be. Speak or sing your request for change into a brightly colored feather (get colored feathers from a craft store). Dance around the fire with your feather while singing or speaking the chant, building the energy. Get loud! When it reaches its peak, throw the feather into the fire. Stay with the energy for a moment then stomp your feet to set it or sit directly on the earth and ground.

From the fire the Phoenix rises!
Flames of change my life transform!
Strength is gained from every crisis!
From my pain wisdom is born!

I am at the age where I can no longer dance around a fire as I used to, nor can I get down on the ground (or should I say get *up* from the ground) for these rituals. I sit where I am comfortable enough to be able to focus completely on the work at hand and imagine my youthful self dancing, jumping around wildly, and gracefully getting up and down at will. If you put your whole self into your imaginings, it is very real and effective.

Persevere to Prevail

I used the following to keep myself going when I thought I couldn't, for whatever reason. Sometimes, we need a little help.

To be sturdy and strong as a persistent vine. This chant came to me during a loved one's struggle with depression and an extraordinarily stressful situation that took such a toll, they were considering ending it all. I put the chant in a place where anyone would see it, including this person. I didn't point it out since no one had asked for my help. The person ultimately worked through some of their difficulties and are still here, actively engaged in finding some serenity. To be clear, I don't know if they ever actually used my chant. I didn't ask. None of my business. But, having said that, the energy pattern of words holding intent can influence an environment in general, not just individuals. It is possible this person took in the focus of the chant by osmosis. Yet another reason to really watch our words.

I have also used this chant for myself (and just the title of this chant as a shortcut affirmation) when struggling under the weight of disappointment. It has proven to be very effective. Others who saw this incantation have said its energy was strengthening to them.

Hold on to life like a persistent vine.
Hold on to any hopeful sign.
Cling to peace and don't let go.
Survive, endure, prevail, and grow.
Cling to justice, truth entwines.
Hold on to life like a persistent vine.

I have struggled with confidence my entire life. It requires some diligence on my part. The following spell has been very helpful...

I banish fear that hinders me!
I speak this spell three times three!
Out fear! Out doubt! Uncertainty!
Then quick and clear my wit will be!
Now quick! Now clear!
Now confident me!

Removing Obstacles

When starting your day seems like you are running an obstacle course, you can say something like this with authority to those obstacles, be it things, people, or pets…

Stand aside,
Clear the way!
Let me stride
On through my day!

Which Way Confusion

The *Three Feathers Charm* is actually a type of simple divination. It's similar to flipping a coin, but much cooler. Take your time formulating your question. Not sure if you should keep your job or quit? Not sure if your relationship is over? Not sure if you should move or stay in your present home? Make your question as clear as possible. Whatever feather lands closest to you is your answer. If more than one land together, think about what other intent might be influencing your question. Hint: don't try this in a strong wind.

You can use any three items for this, like twigs, small stones, acorns, even toothpicks. Use what you've got. Enchant them with possible answers and let them do their work!

Three feathers I cast before me.
Into the air I throw.
Each one that lands
Holds truth for me
About which way to go.
The brown one says to stay.
The white one says to fly away.
The black one says I know (already know the answer).

Of course, you can substitute whatever three colored feathers you want. I used feathers I found on the ground and then returned them to their approximate places. It is illegal to possess migratory bird feathers. This is an opportunity to enlist bird allies if you are proficient at feather identification.

Changing the Vibe

Sometimes I get stuck in a rut. We all have been there. No one is immune. So, it's time to shift the vibe. I came up with a couple of spells that have proven very helpful to me.

The Butter Churn

I have a butter churn from the early 1900s. I actually use it to make butter occasionally and this is what I chant as I churn, especially if I need some help from the goddess Rosmerta in making a change. You need not scour antique stores for one of these. There are several different sizes and styles available online if you want a functional one. But there are also many different versions of dollhouse-size ones for as little as a couple of dollars.

I want to point out here that *you don't need an actual butter churn* to use this charm. Churning butter requires mostly an up-down motion to slosh the cream around. That motion separates the liquid from the fat in the cream and pulls together the particles of that fat into what we call butter.

This transformation can work magically for us in several different ways. For instance, if a situation has become a confusing soup and you want clarity to see the truth of the matter, the magical butter churn can separate out the lies and congeal the truth for you. A churn spell can also help to condense the energies to manifest something in your life, pull it out of your pool of imagination, and bring it together into something useful.

So, any kind of up-down, side-to-side repetitive sloshing motion used while visualizing your idea or desire taking shape out of the "universal cream" of possibilities would work.

It takes some effort and commitment to make decent butter. This energy put towards realizing your goal is what drives the spell.

It is also important to note, if the butter is not properly maintained upon completion, it will go rancid. If the churning wasn't thorough enough, it will go rancid even quicker.

A quick word about Rosmerta. She is one of my favorite goddess forms. Rosmerta was a Celtic, Gaulish, and eventually Roman goddess of abundance and fertility. She was known as the Great Provider. One of Her symbols was the butter churn which has been associated with the cauldron, most often a symbol of transformation.

Oh, Lady of the butter churn,
Rosmerta, make my fortune turn!
Churn, churn, this spell I make!
Separate the truth from fake!
Intent and will and fortitude,
Will manifest the greater good!

It can be used individually or in groups large or small.

Blanket Spell

When an individual or group is trying to exist in a state of confusion, and under unfortunate influence, this spell is effective, but only if done with confidence and conviction. More than one person speaking this spell together, of course, adds to its strength. It works best on small groups. When used on many small groups, especially at the same time, its influence begins to jump, unbidden, to others (think hundredth monkey effect).

I call for a Blanket of Clarity
Cast through all influences
To settle calmly over minds
To relieve fear and reveal courage.

Finding Peace

This next one speaks for itself. I have used it personally, with friends, and in large groups. One can feel it shift the energies of people as they are using it. It can be sung or spoken. Using arm and hand motions as if sending out and pulling back as the tides do, sets up a rocking motion that induces a light trance and enhances the power of the experience. Chant or sing many times through and then gradually reduce voice to a whisper and pull that peace into your center. Once you start the chant or song, you might find you don't want to stop. It's a great way to settle yourself down if feeling anxious, angry, or upset.

In my soul peace grows
And from my heart it flows.
Out into the land
And back to me again.

In my soul peace grows
And from my heart it flows.
Like a calming tide
With this I will abide.

What is one thing you would like to change most in your life? What is one imaginative way to start the process?

5) And Away We Go!

These little charms have never failed me. I have used them even when I was a passenger in someone else's vehicle. In those cases, I just do them silently.

On the Road

For the first one, I add a gesture. I point up with the index finger of my power hand and swirl it three times clockwise, then point strongly straight ahead. Then, put that hand back on the steering wheel, of course.

This little charm cleared the way for me to merge onto expressways every single time!

Swift, safe, and easy access
My whole journey long!

When my husband was alive, he wanted to be the one driving if we were going somewhere. He considered himself the safer driver…and he was right. I always felt safe with him behind the wheel. After he died, I missed that. So, I made a small charm with some of his ashes inside. This, I kept tied to the rear-view mirror. This way, he was with me every time I drove, still protecting me. I asked his spirit first, of course. It has saved me from impossible-to-avoid crashes more than once! I made one for my grandson with the same results.

This next one I used often when the weather was dicey or I had to travel in the dark.

Earth, keep me on the road!
Air, let me see clearly!
Fire, light my way in the dark!
Water, keep the way, fairly!

When traveling in unfamiliar places (cities, forests, seas, etc.), I address the seen and unseen beings that reside there in this manner. Also, it's usually helpful to engage your allies in times such as these. You know, having your friends make introductions for you.

I respect you.
I intend you no harm.
Allow me to pass
With no harm to me!

Where Do I Park?

At the suggestion of a friend, I also have a couple of parking charms!

Close and easy parking
In this journey, just for me!

And my favorite, calling on Abeona, a Roman goddess of traveling forth to a destination,

Abeona, bless my journey's end,
Make parking close and space defend!

What was something that happened on a trip that could have used a bit of magic?

6) How Do You Feel?

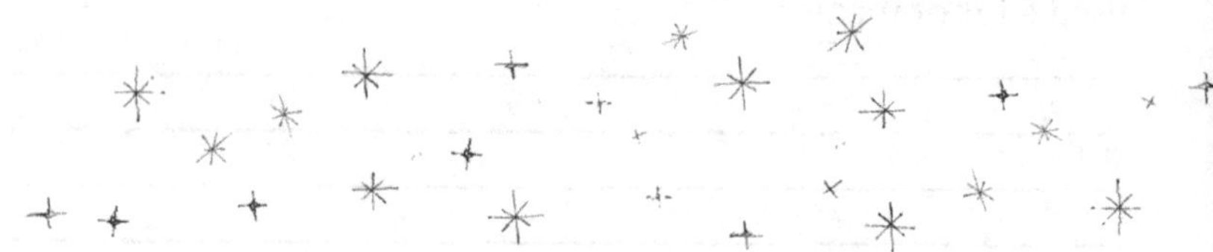

My wisewoman training taught me that it is disrespectful and wrong to try to heal someone unless they ask to be healed. Our definition of healing might not be the same as theirs and *their* definitions are none of our business. They must be in agreement with the idea of being healed for it to work, because their body *heals itself* once it feels it has permission and support. Then, they are motivated to ask for it. But we are not to decide what part needs the healing or what that process will look like. Their pattern reaches out to find the intent pattern of the one who could direct the appropriate energy for their need. Healing often is invisible to others. We look for the obvious showy results, but it is a very personal, internal, and sometimes invisible process.

When asked to help someone heal and we have agreed to do that, then we must trust the process we use and leave the interpretation of the results up to the one who asked for it. Sometimes, just being able to ask for healing is healing in itself. Sometimes, a person asks for healing and that is not what they want at all, but it's part of the process for them to get what they really want.

I had a person once ask me for healing from a serious injury because he was in so much pain. I worked energy to mitigate the pain, while doctors worked to repair the injury. He experienced relief from the pain and the injury started to heal. As soon as his life began to normalize again, he did what the doctors told him not to do and re-injured himself. Again, he asked for help. Again, he experienced relief and healing. But again, he re-injured himself. Many times he put himself through this cycle. It started to become apparent to his loved ones, those helping him, and eventually himself, that he wanted to be taken care of like the ones he had taken care of most of his life. He was getting healing for his heart at the expense of his body.

Friendly Healers

Healing helpers aren't always who you would expect and can be found in the most mundane places when the need arises. Trust your intuition and the magic.

The Pain Stone

My main "go to" tool for this kind of work is a robin-egg-sized, black, volcanic stone a friend gave me. It is a part of a large collection of stones that have found me over the years, and each one helps me in a different way. As soon as I held it in my hand, I knew it would work for me to alleviate pain. Now, stones have been some of my greatest allies since I was small. They regularly communicate with me by showing little movies of what they know across their surfaces for me to see. They are extremely accurate in the information they give me. I will say here, the different types of information my stones give me is completely different than what any book I've read says. So, I follow this rule. I will always ask the stone, not the book. Whatever a stone tells me it is good for, I will believe.

This particular stone showed an image of me gently rubbing it over someone's skin in a circular motion to relieve pain. I tried it and it worked. I am sure that there are many other stones out there, possibly in someone's driveway, that will do the same thing for the right person. If you want to have a pain stone, go to an area where there are a lot of stones. Maybe an old streambed or on the rough edge of a lake. Ask the stones to show you which one would work this way for you. Be patient. Go take a short walk away and then come back. If a particular stone seems to stand out from the rest, that might be the one. Try it out. If it doesn't work, it might be trying to tell you it will help you with something else.

Here is how I work with mine. I keep it in a little bag when I'm not using it. When I need it, I take it out, greet it (always greet your allies), and hold it for a minute or so to warm it up while I tell it what we are about to do. I tell the stone the person's name. Then, I hold the stone in the open palm of my right hand and gently move it in a counterclockwise motion over the area of pain either lightly on their skin or in their aura. Sometimes, I hold it still over the painful spot. I don't think about it; I just rely on the stone and the person's body to make those decisions. In other words, I tune into the person's body and my stone and then move intuitively. I found it helpful to engage the person in light conversation to distract them from the process, or I chant or sing one of the healing charms listed here to quell their anxiety which can disrupt the effect.

After the stone has completed its work, I wash it under cold, running water. The colder, the better and the more forceful the stream of water is, the better. Water is an ally of mine, so I talk to it as I hold the stone under it. I say three times,

Water, wash (person's name) pain
Down the drain!
Down the drain!
Down the drain!

I then dry the stone off, thank it, and put it back in its bag.

Pain Pillow

Because of chronic, severe ear infections as a young child, my oldest daughter was very familiar with pain. One very challenging day when nothing seemed to soothe my child's suffering, I was desperate to provide her with some relief. I had been sewing accent pillows to decorate our sofa at the time. As I looked around helplessly for something to offer her, my eyes settled on a small chenille pillow I had just made. I instantly could picture her laying her painful ear down on this pillow, hopefully helping gravity drain the ear and relieve some pressure. Silently, I told the pillow it just *had* to work for my daughter. To my daughter, I said, "This is a magical pain pillow. If you lay down with this under your ear, you will feel better." It worked for her when hot or cold compresses didn't do the trick! Draining was possible because she laid still, comforted by her new friend, Pain Pillow. Relief from pain was possible because she trusted me and at her tender age of three, she trusted the magic.

Pain Pillow soon became a family tradition as each new scrape, sting, tummy-ache, and ear infection visited my three children. The first step in any first aid incident was to grab Pain Pillow. Over the years, it became threadbare and lumpy from a zillion washes, but it still worked. Sadly, one year when my children were young adults, we lost Pain Pillow to a fire. It had become a member of our family, providing comfort and healing for my children for many years. We mourned.

(Side note here, when an object that has been enchanted is no longer usable, the "soul" or magic you have embodied it with can be released back to Spirit. The enchanted object is allowed to die and can be mourned.)

Magic Water

When my other daughter came to me with a headache one day, I suggested she lie down, but she wasn't having that. So, I got her a glass of water and told her it was magic water that would take headaches away. All she had to do was drink it and stay quiet for a little while. Of course, it worked. She was probably a little dehydrated. But now, water was her ally. When Pain Pillow wasn't available, she knew she could count on Magic Water. There is where the magic lies. My children were shocked when they found out that other families didn't have pain pillows or magic water!

Our Lady Comes

The following original charms were inspired by old Appalachian healing charms I learned decades ago from the Witch Queen of Toledo, the Lady Circe, and Orion Foxwood, Rootworker, Seer, and Appalachian Conjure Man.

I say one of these charms as I lay my hands gently on the subject or on their aura. Though the laying on of hands is effective by itself, the words focus the intent clearly and concisely for both participants. For the one directing the healing, the words remind them they are not the one doing the actual healing. For the one who has asked for healing, the charm redirects their attention from their pain or illness to the comfort and cadence of the words, which produces a light trance state. This helps the person to accept the possibility of being healed and thus gives "permission" for the body to heal itself. The pattern of the rhythm and rhyme of the charm connects easily to the pattern of the laying on of hands because they share the same intent. This combination of intent patterns connects to the pattern generated by the person's willingness to be healed. All of these factors make for a powerful surge of restorative energy.

The term, Lady, used in these charms, refers to the Goddess.

The first one was inspired by the tarot card for strength. The second one was inspired by my vision of divine light rising like the sun in each of us when it is called on to bring a sense of well-being and peace.

As our Lady tames the wild beast,
So She tames the pain!
As Her hand lays down on (name),
All discomfort wanes!

Here's my favorite:

Then from the Dawn
Our Lady came
To bring the balm,
To ease the pain.
Upon (name)'s brow
Her touch is laid
And from Her heart
A healing made!

Three Words of Power

I wrote these for both in-person work and remote work. The charms intentionally exude power from the words chosen and the phrasing which leaves no room for doubt in the mind of the healing worker or the receiver.

As you may have noticed, these and many other spells and charms in this book can have interchangeable or substituted words, depending on need.

The Great Mother stands before (name)
Who is suffering with sickness and pain.
She speaks three words of power.
You will heal! You will heal! You will heal!
And it is done!

The Great Mother stands before (name)
Who is suffering in blood and pain.
She speaks three words of power,
You will live! You will live! You will live!
And it is done!

The Great Mother stands before (name)
Who exists in sadness and fear.
She speaks three words of power,
You will thrive! You will thrive! You will thrive!
And it is done!

The Great Mother stands before (name)
Who has been bit by fire.
She speaks three words of power,
You will heal! You will heal! You will heal!
And it is done!

Spirit of the Light

Once when I was feeling desperate, alone, and beaten down, I called to the Gods (how I define Spirit) for relief, and this happened. I have used this many times for myself and others who have come to me wanting help.

Take three breaths. Imagine yourself surrounded by the four

elements. You notice a glow high above you. Open your arms up as you call to the Spirit of Divine Light in all Its aspects to bless you with pure energy from Source!

I call to the power
Of the Spirit of the Light!
Rise like the dawning of the sun.
Shine in me, shine in me!
Radiate the brilliance of life!

The glow intensifies into a single beam of pure white light, descending in through the top of your head. Make room for it in your body. Feel its brightness dissolve unwanted, unneeded attachments. Feel it fill every part of you, lighting up each and every cell until you are glowing. Feel it revitalize you, strengthen you. Now, radiate some of that light out through your skin. Fill your aura. It becomes a shield against uninvited energies that would cling to you. Keep the rest in your inner temple for when you need extra energy.

The beam of light recedes back to Source now but is always available to you.

Give thanks to the Divine in whatever aspect you know. If you ever want to pull that powerful light back in, call to the Divine as you know it and guide the light into your Inner Temple with your hands. You can radiate it out again at will.

Give thanks to the Spirit of the Light.

(The Spirit of the Light can also be added to the Elemental verses in Part I of this book as the fifth element.)

For a healthy cleansing, here is a short little chant that works well when dancing in the rain or around a fire or in the rain around a fire!

Fire and Water!
Sun and Sea!
Cleanse and Bless!
So shall it be!

This one is fun to do with children on a hot, sunny day in summer with the sprinkler on.

Bless You!

This blessing is open for interpretation. For some, having truth as a constant companion may be very challenging if they are prone to lying. And if they are the hateful kind, they probably would not enjoy being covered in a cloak of love! Then again, this blessing could begin a healing process.

May Truth be your constant Companion
And Spirit, your beacon of Light.
Courage, be your Staff on your journey

And Love your Cloak in the night.

This one makes a great morning or evening prayer. It is also very soothing when said during times of great stress.

May the blessings of all the earthly elements be upon me (him, them, her, you).
May the stars look kindly down upon me (him, them, her, you).
May the ways of the universe be open to my (his, their, her, your) higher good.

What kinds of healing have you experienced?

7) Self Boosters

The following verses I have used as affirmations said to myself in a mirror or chanted quietly as part of my meditative practice. I sometimes chant them while walking my dog. It keeps me focused on good, helpful energy of my choosing and prevents me from getting caught up in any contentious energy floating around the neighborhood. I have noticed I can't worry about things and chant these at the same time. Invent ones that exactly fit you!

Love and Be Loved

When feeling down, sometimes it's hard to think we are loved. We are so busy finding fault in our thoughts and actions, we don't realize we are abandoning ourselves when we need ourselves the most. Then, we really shut down and often can't accept what we need when offered. This affirmation has always been a good reminder to me to stay open to the gifts of our world, while reinforcing boundaries of what we are willing to accept.

I freely love
And accept love in return.
I freely respect
And accept respect in return.
I freely honor
And accept honor in return.
I freely value
And accept value in return.

This one is a reminder to ourselves that we are part of the world, not separate. Therefore, we are never alone. This makes a great focus for meditation.

I am the light in my life.
My light shines into the world.
I am part of the turning Wheel.
I help keep the Wheel in motion!

And this is the one I use most just because it feels so good. It also makes a great focus for meditation.

The light of my being shines.
It shines from the core of my soul.
A beacon in the darkness.

The light of my being shines.
It is my connection to Source.
Source is the light of my being.

Here is another one for yourself or someone you care about that needs reminding.

You are not alone
Nor will you ever be.
No matter where we look
We see you and you see we.
The world is big
But made of smaller parts.
Each part is put together
Of even smaller parts.
We are actually one
From the first to very last.
We are the bigger picture
Just in miniature cast.
One person plus one person,
Going on and on.
Everything works in tandem
One for all and all for one.
Any acts against you

Are acts against us all.
And if you lose your balance
We will break your fall.
You are not alone
No matter what you do.
We are not alone
For we are here with you.

I Can Handle It

If I know my day is going to be challenging, I will chant this in the morning as I'm getting ready. This works well as a chant to go into a meditative state.

I am peaceful, patient,
Compassionate and calm.

I hope you will create your own affirmations and meditations. That process can take a while and that's okay. The creative process is a powerful meditation in its own right. And as time goes by, as your needs change, these will change too. You will modify them and create new ones. It will become a dynamic, evolving river, flowing through your psyche, nourishing you as you grow.

What would you like to hear that would help you feel stronger, smarter, more confident? Try turning it into a chant you can say while taking a shower, driving to work, or walking the dog.

PART III

ENDINGS AND BEGINNINGS

1) Leaving

Staying behind when someone moves on beyond the veil is such an intense, personal experience. Every heart truly grieves alone. All I have to offer are two pieces I wrote to help me deal with my grief and honor my loved one who left. You, dear reader, may use them if they speak to you, or let them inspire you to create from your own heart.

The first one is also in Part I of this book.

Thank you for the gift of your life now passed.
May your next life be better than your last.
Release to the Light, blessed spirit.

This second offering is derived from a memorial service I wrote and conducted where ashes were released.

We release from our grasp the sacred soul of (name)
into the Light of Spirit.
We release from our grasp (name's) body back to the element of
Earth from which it was made, and from which new life is made.
(Ashes were released.)
Thank you, (name), for being part of our lives.
Blessed be the Sojourner and blessed be the Journey.

2) Hello, Are You There?

I believe we leave our bodies and shift into a different dimension when we die. We can still communicate, however. We become ancestors for the people we care about. Not all ancestors are willing to reconnect to this world through interaction, but the ones who are willing can become our best allies. They know what it is to be human. They truly understand the basic struggles we have in this life. They not only can show us the past, but from their viewpoint, I believe they can see the bigger picture; thus they could give us hints of our future as well. Just like creating and maintaining other alliances, respect and reciprocity are the most important elements. There are many ways we can initiate contact or take part in interactions with them and satisfy their needs as well as our own. Here are some ideas.

To create an altar of remembrance, decide what you want to remember about them, or what they have indicated they want to be remembered for. Now, put those things or symbols of those things in one place and don't use that space for anything else. Lighting a candle on an altar is a traditional way of honoring an ancestor. If they enjoyed coffee, place a cup of coffee on the altar once in a while, maybe when you have your morning coffee. If you can't find anything to put on the altar, write their name on a candle and when you light it, repeat their name, or even just write their name on a piece of paper and put that in the space. You will remember them every time you see it.

Here is a story about remembrance.

Grandpa's Favorite Chair

I had been called on to handle a potential haunting many years ago, by a young family with a baby and a new (to them) apartment. The place was very small, so when they moved in, they turned the dining room into a nursery and placed the crib in the corner near the room's only window. The baby, who had previously been a good sleeper, now wouldn't sleep. She would cry and scream and try to climb out of the crib. She would only settle down when taken to another part of the apartment. The mother stated that the light in the dining room/nursery now was always dim, as if in shadow, even when the curtains were opened or the ceiling light was on. Both she and her husband began to feel on edge whenever they were in that room. They started to think that maybe the place was haunted.

I took a friend along who also had some experience with hauntings because we didn't know what we might find. The place was just as they had described it, dim and stuffy.

As my friend and I explored the apartment, the spirit of an elderly gentleman made himself known. He got right up in my face and demanded to know who these people were who had taken up residence in *his* apartment. He insisted we move the crib right away because it was where his rocking chair was. He said he had been yelling at the baby and the parents to get out so he could sit down in his favorite chair.

He always sat there by the window to wait and watch for his wife to come home. He couldn't sit in it anymore because the crib was in the way and there just wasn't enough room anymore!

We talked to him for quite a while and explained that he had died and no longer had a body, so no longer needed an apartment or a chair. We told him all about the young family who had moved in because they had nowhere else to go. He shared that he and his wife had been Holocaust survivors and when they came to America, they found this little apartment and had lived there ever since but never had children. As we talked, it became clear that his wife had preceded him in death, and he was very lonely. We managed to convince him that he could go be with her and let this young family have the apartment. We reminded him that he and his wife had been young once, just like this couple. He agreed, and we did a little ceremony to help him and his wife find each other, so he could go and be with her.

He had one request before he left. He wanted someone to remember him. He was afraid no one would know he and his wife had ever existed. They had been the only survivors of their families, and his rocking chair was his only connection to this life. If he gave it up, he would be gone forever. He just wanted his life to count.

Of course, his chair was no longer there physically. It

disappeared when the apartment was cleared out after his death. We explained that when he rejoined his wife, he would no longer need the rocking chair. The family promised to honor him and his wife and the courageous life they shared. We promised he would be remembered. The family agreed to place a little table under the window with a candle on it and light it once a year on the deceased couple's anniversary. We wrote their names on the candle. He was now satisfied that his last wish had been granted. He even stated he and his wife wouldn't mind watching over the new couple and their baby since they had had no children of their own. When he saw his wife in the distance, he faded away. They had become ancestors.

I share this story to illustrate two important points. One, the little table with the candle became an altar to remember this courageous couple. Very simple. Altars need not be fancy. They exist to serve a purpose. An altar is a place set aside to be a sacred space for not only worshiping, honoring, and communing with deities but also for remembering and working with those who have gone before, our ancestors.

Anything can be an altar. Even the elderly gentleman's rocking chair could have been an altar. It was his favorite chair and when others would see it, they would remember him. I have several altars in my house, two of which are for my ancestors. The largest one has two parts, one for each side of my family. Each part is full of photos of those particular ancestors.

Anything can go on an altar, as long as there is intention with it. When I was little, I would present my mother with a little hand-picked bouquet of violets and lily of the valley on her birthday. She has been gone for many years now, but I still go out and pick that little bouquet and place it in front of her picture on the altar every year. I give a nod to all my ancestor photos whenever I walk past them and when I dust, I greet each ancestor as I move their picture out of the way. I can add items that I know they like, such as their favorite flowers or even a live plant. My altars provide a place where I can talk with my ancestors to ask for help or to thank them for assistance.

The second point of my story, if you haven't already guessed, is creating and maintaining an alliance. Placing items on an ancestor altar can help encourage them to communicate, such as pieces of their jewelry, awards, favorite tools, even items of their clothing. Anything that would be holding some of their energy, links to their past. In the case of the deceased couple, just a small sacred space and the promise of a candle lit once a year encouraged the gentleman to offer to watch over the young family.

Sitting undisturbed in front of my ancestor altar and talking to them as if having a conversation has worked best for me. Then, remaining quiet and relaxed opens a space for them to reply. It is always a good idea to journal your conversations for later.

Ancestors as allies are important. They not only have wisdom accrued just by living, but they know your family history for generations back. Family ancestors are connected to you by your bloodline, so you probably have inherited some of their traits. They can be good advisors and can add their energies to your workings...if you have fostered or continued a relationship with them. There are culture-specific holidays for honoring ancestors all over the world and most have culture-specific rituals, prayers, and songs, but they all have one thing in common. Just because these ancestors have left this life doesn't mean they aren't still alive in our hearts and minds and still have something to offer to our lives today. With ancestors as allies, it is even possible to work through unhealthy family issues passed down from one generation to the next.

My family of origin didn't have anything special with which to honor our ancestors, other than old family stories and photos. But as a child, I was very intrigued by the fact that my parents had parents who had parents...you get the idea. And they all lived through history. My father knew many of his family's stories going back generations and I loved to hear them. Now, I have told them to my children, grandchildren, and great-grandchildren. Storytelling is a profound way to honor ancestors. Nothing keeps history alive more than knowing that a member of your own family lived hundreds of years ago and survived the plague, or was a knight during the Crusades, or crossed the Delaware with George Washington!

My work with ancestors has evolved over the years. At various times, I have used chants, drumming, singing, and prayer to communicate with them. Here are the ones I like the best and use the most.

You Are Formally Invited

Give your ancestors an invitation to visit. It is important to have some boundaries in place and also focused intent as to which ancestor(s) you want contact with at the time. It is healthy to also have time boundaries. Contact can go on and on while you lose track of time. Both of these invites can be done by one person or a group.

Ancestors, I'm calling you!
From the stones
And through the wind
They whisper in your ear.
From your bones
And through your skin
You feel them when they're near.
Ancestors are always near!
I'm calling you, Ancestors!

This next one I did with a group of friends on Samhain night. It is a call and response chant where one person does the call and the rest do the response. It can be lots of fun, especially if you all are shaking rattles or bones. I strongly recommend clean and dried chicken bones or fake bones from a Halloween shop or small chunks of wood you can paint to look like bones.

The first two lines are whispered. Then, the following lines get progressively louder. This chant is best when repeated over and over, getting louder each time. It is great to do while circling a cauldron or a fire ring. You can share something like this with your children to make a family tradition for Halloween.

Ancestors coming! (call)
Rattle the bones! (response)
Ancestors dancing! (call)
Rattle the bones! (response)
Ancestors singing! (call)
Rattle the bones! (response)
Rattle the bones! (response)
Rattle the bones! (response)

Sharing drink and food on an altar is a big part of many traditions. It is always polite to provide nourishment for guests, and ancestors are no different. It is generally believed that they will consume the energy from the food and drink and leave the physical remains to be disposed of as they no longer have any nutritional value. It is very important to remember that every calling and visit requires a thank you when the interaction is finished. A simple thank you and goodbye is all that is necessary, but this part can be as elaborate as you like. Here is one that I use.

To you, no more to earth are tied
And from beyond the veil still guide,
Thank you for your loving grace
And time we shared in sacred space.
Your wisdom valued, your story told.
May our connection always hold.
I say farewell as you depart
With love and trust from heart to heart.

Rites of Honor
This one is a short rite honoring their contributions.

By bones and stones,
By blood and soil,
The thread of life
Through time does coil.
Ancestors live!

They hold the line.
From life to death,
The thread they wind.
From death to life,
They weave for me
Their lessons gain eternity!

This next one is a calling, a rite of honor, and a statement of grateful farewell; a whole ritual in itself. This rite came to me almost fully formed while walking through the woods over several evenings one autumn, verse by verse. It is now my yearly devotion to those who came before me.

The concept of ancestors is very important to me. I am aware of the many lessons that come from old family stories and the glimpses of history that small family traditions have given me. The turmoil both sides of my family endured generations ago, being on opposing sides of wars, struggling to survive famine, epidemics, and natural disasters, long journeys by sea and on foot, only strengthened their resolve and fortitude. Enough of them survived to allow another generation to be born…for *me* to be born.

I feel their strength in me when I'm faced with a crisis. I still ask my long-gone grandmother for advice when I'm following one of her recipes, and I can still hear my father's words when I make his family's old southern healing salve for cuts and scrapes.

Singing lullabies from across the sea that have been passed down from mother to mother for at least seven generations help keep me connected to my roots and as they are passed from me to my great-grandchildren, the connections move through the present and into the future in an unbroken line.

The Ancestor Song[1]

Into the mist I call to you
By light of fire I sing your name.
The blood within like a river flows
Through rock and wood and wind and rain.
Still, through the dark I reach for you!
The blood, it speaks to ancient ear.
Wake up, Ancestors, hear my call!
My need is great, come near! Come near!

Then from the mist a whisper dim
Assuring words my heart does hear.
"Oh, we have not abandoned you,
We hold you close. No need to fear.
To carry forward all your dreams,

1 Reproduced with permission from Bell, Book, and Canto

You must remember who you are
And honor those who've gone before

We stand together near and far."
In peace and loving gratitude
I hold their wisdom deep inside
And from my heart I bid farewell
To my revered ancestral guides.

Acknowledging one's ancestors need not be formal. Reverence can be paid by passing along the old stories, recipes, holiday traditions, and of course, family photos. Anything that reminds you of a deceased family member or ancestor can be a connecting point and communication channel.

They are such a rich source of knowledge, wisdom, and love. They can assist you in energy work and finding hidden information. Sit down and have a cup of tea or a drink with them. Tell them what's on your mind. Then, pay attention to your dreams and random references to them in your waking life. Listen to song lyrics. Answers can hide anywhere!

Sometime after my husband passed away, I spent quite a while agonizing over the decision to start dating again. After a night of talking to him about my inability to move on with my life, I woke up the next morning with a song running around in my head. You know what I'm talking about...you just can't shake that song, no matter what you do! It was a song from my college days and one I really disliked. I couldn't figure out why I kept humming it. Until I paid attention to the words. "If you can't be with the one you love, love the one you're with." Question answered.

How would you ask one of your ancestors to come and share some wisdom? How would you thank them?

3) Arriving

Each person has their own journey, and we aren't privy to that. As much as we might want to, we don't have the final say about someone's destiny. But who doesn't want the best for a new baby? Making up rhymes on the spot can be so much fun when done in lighthearted moments! Here is one I came up with when meeting a minutes-old newborn.

Well, bless your head
And bless your feet
And all from here to there.
May your mind be sharp,
Your body strong,
And life without a care.

The old nursery rhymes I grew up with are terribly outdated, having been written hundreds of years ago. They don't have any connection to modern life. Other than for entertainment, their value was that they were teaching rhymes for their day. So, be the new Mother Goose and make up your own. It is so much fun to create a little ditty with a toddler!

When my children were very young, we created a goodnight song together that we would sing every night once they were in bed. In the song, we sang good night to each other, then other family members, even distant relatives, then other people we knew...you get the idea. We lived on our farm in those days, so we sang goodnight to every animal in the barn, of course. Anything to keep from going to sleep, you know. I just kept singing softer and slower until one by one, they fell asleep. A lullaby. A sleeping charm. Magic. Sometimes, though, I was the one who fell asleep first! The combination of the rhythm, the repetitive words, and the tune creates a trance-like state that induces relaxation. Add your silent intent for good sleep, and you have a magical working.

Create other little songs with children to keep them engaged in whatever the activity is. Just hold your intent in your mind or put it in the words. Intent can ride on a sing-song voice. Have a diaper changing song, a bathing song, a breakfast, lunch, or dinner song, etc.

Listen to young children playing. They make up little songs and charms naturally, enchanting their toys to bring them alive.

Children live in their magical selves until society claims them. It's still inside them, though. It's still inside *you*. Ask your inner child.

Did you have an enchanted toy when you were a child? How did you make it come alive?

PART IV

THE TEMPLE OF THE SACRED FLAME

I will end this little book by guiding you to create your Inner Temple, a sacred place inside you for your soul. A place to go when you need to escape the craziness of life. A place of respite in which to gather your strengths. You can even live your whole life from there. You will be centered and grounded all the time!

Gather a pencil and maybe some crayons. Settle yourself away from distractions. Take a few slow, deep breaths, and think about what your temple would look like. On the blank pages in this part of the book, randomly draw dots. Lots of them. They represent particles of potential energy. Remember them from the Connect-the-Dots section? Now, connect some of those dots with lines of intention to design your temple. You can use more pages for your intent patterns of different parts of your temple, if you like.

Be thorough and detailed. What shape will it be? How big or small? Solid walls or open sides? Windows, doors? Remember, this is *your* temple. For *your* soul. There is no standard to follow for this. Make it exactly the way *you* want. What kind of floor will it have, or maybe no floor at all? Does it have a roof, or is it open to the sky?

Think about furnishings, too. What would you like to have in your temple? What colors will you choose? Will there be music? Are there any flowers or other plants? Keep adding detail to your drawing, either on the pages or in the fertile ground of your mind until it has everything you want. The more you interact with it, the stronger your lines of intention become and the more real your temple becomes.

Make a place for the sacred flame in the center. This flame is made of the same divine spark that animates you. It feeds your soul. This is your spiritual energy center.

Once your temple is completely finished and you have designated a place for your sacred flame, go deep inside yourself and make room for your temple. Then lift the energy essence of your temple off the paper or out of your mind. Just scoop it up with your hands. Now place it into your body. You can push it in right through your skin. Make sure it is in the right place. Make adjustments as needed. Breathe deeply. Feel it in there. Now, ride your breaths down and go inside your temple. Do you feel safe? If not, make changes until you do. Add anything else you might want in there. You can dance, sing, or sleep, anything you want to do inside your temple with no interference. No one can alter your experience of your temple because no one knows it exists except you. No one knows where to find it. Your soul is untouchable in your temple. Regardless of what is going on around you or with your body, your soul is indestructible.

Return to your temple whenever you feel drained, to be recharged, revived, reset, restored. This is the place to get yourself centered and grounded. A place to figure things out and find the strengths you need from your unlimited storehouse to face the world. This is where your magic lives. Your sacred flame feeds the divine spark in the core of you and keeps your magic alive.

It is up to you to tend your sacred flame. If your flame is struggling, call down the Spirit of the Light addressed earlier in this book to radiate down into your temple and feed your sacred flame. You take care of the flame, and the flame takes care of you.

We are connected to everything and the magic flows freely through it all. We use it even when we aren't aware of it. It's the whole pattern thing. It's just how it works. So, why not use it intentionally? It will keep you young. Look at the world with the eyes of a child but respond to the world with wisdom.

THE TEMPLE OF THE SACRED FLAME

BONADEA'S BOOK OF EVERYDAY ENCHANTMENTS